URBAN
sanctuaries

STEPHEN ANDERTON

URBAN *sanctuaries*

PEACEFUL HAVENS FOR THE CITY GARDENER

MITCHELL BEAZLEY

To CL, CB–H and CPH, who are teaching me how to see.

First published in 2001 by Mitchell Beazley,
an imprint of Octopus Publishing Group Ltd,
2–4 Heron Quays, London E14 4JP
New edition 2006

ISBN 1 84533 241 5

A CIP catalogue copy of this book is available from
the British Library

Deputy Art Director Vivienne Brar
Project Editor Michèle Byam
Design Lovelock & Co
Editor Richard Dawes
Production Controller Nancy Roberts
Picture Researcher Jenny Faithfull
Indexer Laura Hicks

Set in Foundry

Printed and bound in China by
Toppan Printing Company Limited

contents

introduction

Sanctuary. Retreat. Getting away from it all. These things are the dream of city dwellers. Perhaps the ultimate sanctuary in a city is a peaceful garden, with its powers of rejuvenation and regeneration. Everyone knows the healing properties of a garden, and, with the right planning, a well-designed garden sanctuary can be anybody's.

BELOW Town gardeners have to learn to work with scale. Is this a Brazilian plutocrat's swimming pool with massive primitive sculptures by Roberto Burle Marx, or is ita couple of pebbles on the edgeof a raised pool?

What is the real difference, you might wonder, between designing an urban garden and a country garden? The answer is nothing. Design is always a matter of mass and proportion and momentum. Urban gardens simply work on a smaller scale, because the gardens themselves are generally smaller. But there are huge differences between what people want from an urban garden and what they want from a country garden. The brief to the urban garden designer or the urban gardener is totally different, and the most significant difference is in the relationship of the urban gardener with nature.

Nature, which today we so admire, and which man has always found intensely beautiful, is also a dangerous maelstrom of competing forces. We are just one of those forces. Civilization has sufficiently given us the upper hand to be able to control our environment and make it safer. Now we long for nature's beauty without its dangers, and call that a garden, a sanctuary from man-made and natural dangers.

For as long as there has been civilization and surplus wealth, gardens have been a defence against the natural environment. It is easy for us now to look generously and bravely upon nature, from our world of central heating and health care and pest control. But just a hundred years ago nature was still the great She-bitch. Weather and disease and predators wiped out millions with magnificent coldness, despite our best efforts. The natural world was something to use our ingenuity against, to build walls against. It was a wilderness of potential cruelty, where every straight line, whether part of a country cottage or grand baroque garden, was a victory for civilization, and for human life.

And so developed the great tradition of walled gardens, in Persia and Kashmir and Spain. Renaissance Italy made its great, ordered terraces, and within the walls of monasteries market gardening began, and the tradition of intensive production which was to lead to the great walled gardens of the eighteenth- and nineteenth-century country house.

RIGHT What is natural? Certainly not this contrived, linear planting of wild and garden flowers. And yet there is peacefulness to be found in this garden, drawing on a semi-natural grassland style but bringing artificial line and movement as well – making it a garden, in fact. Nature, like a good designer, has discipline, and uses a few plants generously, to good effect.

Today the relationship with nature is quite different. In industrialized countries the majority of the population has moved from the country into towns. Now we spend most of our life in urban areas, and long again for the countryside. We are tired of cars and asphalt and concrete and sheet metal and flashing lights and noise and fumes. A few of us are even sick of shopping. What we want now is not to protect ourselves from nature, but to retreat into it – or at least into a tamed, ordered version of nature, which is a garden. Whether it is a simple courtyard or a jungle of bananas and bamboo, a garden in the city is the greatest, most improbable, and most unexpected of luxuries. A garden is the place where you can kick off your shoes at the end of the day and say, "Home! Sanctuary!".

But it is not enough, or only at first does it seem enough, to say that our own patch of land, our own garden, is the perfect antidote to urban life. It has to work objectively to be that antidote. It has to be designed to be that antidote, if the pleasure and the relief it brings is to last, once the novelty has worn off. It needs to cater precisely to our personal requirements, and provide those things which soothe us most.

Gardeners find the pleasures of gardening in different ways. For some it is the opportunity to get hands and knees dirty, and to feel some communion with the earth. It is a tactile thing. The physical sensations and satisfactions of working the soil can produce a kind of mental euphoria, if a person has that particular link in the psyche. Why else, after a hard day's digging or an afternoon spent up a ladder thinning trees, do we slump into a hot bath, worn out and blissful at the same time? A little pain and a little pleasure have always been a recipe for success.

Other gardeners take their pleasure by looking on. To them, the pleasure of a garden is found simply by being in it. It is somewhere which has its own order and design, and makes no demands for order from them. It is somewhere already complete, in which a person whose working life involves organizing things and people can switch off. It is such a person's chance to be passive for a change. Half an hour in the garden in the morning – taking breakfast perhaps – or half an hour in the evening – after dark perhaps, with or without lights on – can be all the soul needs to balance its day.

There are other gardeners for whom a garden is just the opposite of passivity. For them it is a chance to play not physical but mental gymnastics.

BELOW *Is this natural? Certainly not. It is an agricultural landscape, managed for timber and shelter and hay. And yet it contains masses of native plants. Between times of activity – to fell trees or cut hay, drive in cattle – this scene is intensely peaceful. It is the rural idyll of managed nature to which many gardeners aspire when they garden in a naturalistic style.*

These are the gardeners who love to plan colour schemes and to play with careful compositions of potted plants on a terrace, or to collect three dozen kinds of echeverias in pots, or to make the garden so jungly with exotics that it begins to look like a snapshot of Borneo. For these gardeners a garden is a workplace, just as much as it is for those who love gardening for the physical exercise. It is their chance to give the orders, to stay on top.

A few people want an urban garden simply to be a room outdoors, a living room under the sky. They want it for all the kinds of things you would normally do indoors – eating, cooking, listening to music, working at a table, reading in comfort, playing games, showering, jumping into a hot tub with some glamorous creature. Or two. It is a perfectly valid way of looking at gardens, however much plantaholic gardeners may disapprove.

All these attitudes to gardening apply as much to gardeners in the country as to those in the town. Everyone knows plant collectors' country gardens, with enough camellias to stage *La Traviata*, or the gardener who installs a hot tub with a perfect view of snow-capped mountains, or makes a meadow with more wild flowers than the hedgerows beyond.

BELOW *Sometimes what matters most to an urban gardener is a sense of space, or, more precisely, a verdant place to be in, with a prospect of some kind. Not all towns offer views such as this one, an enviable mixture of naturalistically planted focus and a long prospect. The plants are an exotic mixture from all over the world. It is the style of planting which makes for a relaxed, natural feeling.*

LEFT *Urban and suburban life can take away every chance of a prospect. Then gardens become inward-looking. This is both a challenge and an opportunity to work in styles which, because of their location, are not obliged to relate to the surrounding countryside but still must be peaceful if they are to serve their purpose. They have to operate as if cars and tarmac and urban noise were a million miles away, elevating the simplest and sometimes most difficult spaces into sanctuaries.*

But country gardeners have nature all around them, and it is there to be enjoyed all the time. In a way this makes gardening harder. Country gardeners have to decide how to achieve a happy transition from the highly organized greenery of a garden to the simpler organization of farmland or to more natural woods, or to that rare thing a genuinely natural landscape.

A country gardener could turn his back on his surroundings and make an inward-looking walled garden. But that would be to avoid the challenge. You have only to look at some of the great eighteenth-century landscape parks to see what can be achieved by addressing the landscape boldly and playing with nature – in their case the creation of vast, idealized, naturalistic versions of the agricultural landscape of rolling pastures, woods, and water. In the country the smallest of gardens may have the grandest of prospects, with a little care and a little focusing of the view. Town gardens are rarely so lucky.

Country gardens may have nature come in to meet them directly, in the form of water. It might be a river running across the bottom of the garden, or a stream rushing through it. A delicious prospect. But what a challenge it is to make a happy transition somewhere along that watercourse from wild water to garden. It would be very strange suddenly to tame that stream into a slow-moving, formal canal, unless you were to cut off all view of its wildness as it enters your land and to create a separate, quieter world in the garden. The great landscape parks made use of canalized rivers and tamed watercourses, turning busy streams into wide, sluggish "rivers", but the overall designs of these creations were on such a vast scale that they could make such ambitious works seem relatively natural.

ABOVE *The great eighteenth-century landscape parks worked on such a large scale that their designers could afford to make the whole landscape a garden, to create an idealized version of the agricultural landscape which filled the entire view. Most of us today garden within artificial or architectural boundaries, making the opportunity for formal, "unnatural" gardening so much greater.*

For a town gardener water is a far more precious and rare commodity. Usually it has to be provided artificially, and in this sense it is not a link with nature so much as a symbol of it.

The country gardener, then, has a perpetual option on making fruitful relations between relatively sympathetic, rural surroundings and the interior of the garden. For the urban gardener things are different. City streets are the antithesis of gardens, and good public parks are all too few. However much an urban gardener may find satisfaction in the physical process of gardening, his garden will also need to be made a sanctuary from his immediate surroundings – from the metallic rumpus of the city – if it is to satisfy the brain as well as the body. Country gardeners can take or leave their surroundings. Urban gardeners must do battle with their surroundings, and make something independent of them or possibly closed off from them, where the pace and atmosphere are completely different from what lies beyond the garden. They must work to make something intrinsically peaceful, with no help from their surroundings.

Gardeners are all different, of course, and every one will have a preference for a different style of gardening. But whatever the style, the way to make a peaceful garden is always to concentrate on simplicity and clarity of design, to concentrate on resolution more than distraction, to find forms which balance more than they jar, to create an oasis of privacy in which you can indulge your pleasures, whatever they may be, to find sounds or silences, and perfumes, too, which bring you closer to a sense of calm, and to combine all these notions into something which offers renewal and refreshment for the urban psyche.

Not a lot to ask? Of course it is. Some gardens never make it. Some offer visual pleasure and provocation, but never peace or harmony. Some offer stylized horticultural perfection but have no soul. Each to his own, I say.

There is another pleasure I have not mentioned. The pleasure of trying – with all your heart and brain – to create a sanctuary suited perfectly to you. The greatest pleasures are often found in the trying. I can offer no short cut to knowing what kind of sanctuary would suit you best. But perhaps I can offer you the inspiration and discipline to make such a sanctuary a reality.

BELOW *The pleasure of a city garden can be in playing with ideas of what is natural and what is artificial. In its way this collection of semi-natural shapes is doing on a smaller scale what was done with landform in a landscape park. Gardening is always a contrivance, however naturalistic you try to make it. Gardeners should accept this premise and work with it, not fight it.*

part one

the body of
the garden

space and scale

Perhaps you already have an urban garden. Perhaps you are about to acquire one. Either way, the first thing to do is to evaluate what exists already, and to see how the garden can be turned into a genuinely peaceful place. The most important thing – and the place to start – is to look at space and scale.

Space comes first. Space, however it is decorated, is what gardens are made of. So look at the shape of the garden as a whole. Not just the part which is currently open space. Imagine the garden open to its boundaries. Would it feel ten times bigger without the planting? Is the sense of spaciousness hugely reduced by trees and shrubs? That may not necessarily be a bad thing, but it has to be what you want.

Think about how the total space relates to the house. Most urban gardens are dominated by the houses they serve, even roof gardens. So it is important at the start to think about how you want that relationship to work. Do you want a seamless transition from space in the house to space in the garden, through sliding doors? Do you want the garden to be a separate, moist world, to step into and leave the house behind? Or do you want both – liveable open space around the house and a hidden sanctum of foliage farther on?

The architecture of the house will also make demands upon your gardening. Visually commanding entrances will ask for a response in the design of the

OPPOSITE Here is a narrow, small garden, with none too wide a path going down the centre to a seating area which maximizes the width. When the plants have grown, as you walk down the path you'll feel like mercury squeezing up a thermometer. And that's good.

RIGHT Three heavy trees make this bed seem tiny and insignificant. Imagine it with three small birch saplings: it would seem so much bigger. The shed would no longer be out of the space, behind trees. It would become a part of it, and its boundary.

RIGHT *A path sneaks off to another part of the garden, or suggests there is more space behind. The scale of the hosta's foliage hiding the path makes the plant leap forward and pushes the path farther back.*

garden, so a grand door case will ask for steps or a vista of some kind, however small. A house which is generous in the scale and quality of its construction may call for correspondingly generous hard landscaping – wide steps and terraces and paths perhaps. The scale of such features might require large paving units such as slabs of sawn stone, rather than something small-scale like brick. Or you might use brick in a grid pattern, to suggest a matrix of larger-scale squares.

The house may be so unappealing that all you want to do is cover it up with a pergola and vines. But whatever its appearance, it has to be made to work with the garden. Ignore it at your peril. A peaceful space will only come from combining the major elements harmoniously and constructively. And the house is invariably one of the biggest elements.

Think about the vertical dimension of the garden. Is it taller than it is wide, like a tube between buildings? If so, do you want to emphasize the height with tapering, soaring shapes which point to the source of light above? Or do you wish to make the garden its own enclosed world of jungle vegetation and ignore all that void above? The choice is yours.

Some gardens, even small ones, have enormous changes of level. Don't see this as necessarily a problem. In the country, flatland gardeners are thoroughly jealous of gardeners with some exciting topography to play with. Why should it not be the same in towns? Only the scale is different. So think about whether you are making the most of changes of level. You may need enough flat space to sit out and eat, but after that, what does it matter if the whole garden is a set of steps or terraces? Make them as complex and as cunning as you like. Terraces are inevitably a man-made construction, and you should feel free to emphasize this as much as you like. Make the hard landscaping speak. If the garden descends to a dark hole, make that the place you want to be. Put a fern jungle in it, or even a hot tub. Or both.

Evaluate the views from the garden. Some gardens have none worth seeing. Others may have a panorama of city roofs which you would be crazy to hide, especially at night. Others – most – will have one architecturally or leafily interesting segment of the view which could be emphasized, but elsewhere only shabbiness which needs screening out. Let your garden breathe by giving it the best of its long prospects, but lose the muddle. Lose the clutter. Focus it.

You can even steal some sense of spaciousness by playing with perspective. City gardeners use mirrors or painted landscapes within a window frame or garden doorway to suggest distance. But you can also play with perspective in

ABOVE *Large random paving slows down the perceived momentum of the path, controlling the atmosphere of the garden. Imagine how bricks laid in line with the direction of the path would speed it up.*

LEFT *Fussy plantings, which here even fills up the centre of the path, can be spatially uninviting, and no greater than the sum of its many horticultural parts. The statue at the end provides a vital contrast of texture, and tells you there is space for you ahead.*

the garden itself. Exaggerate distances by making things which are closer to the eye larger – topiary or a huge vase, perhaps – and by making similar objects farther away progressively smaller. A nearby fat tree trunk leaning across a window or patio creates a sense of dignity and distance. The eye is readily deceived.

Think carefully about the scale of planting within the garden. Mean, narrow borders around the edges of a space do little to make it serene. Better to scrap them and have one decent-sized area of planting and to create a new interest in the surrounding walls themselves, or the fences, with paint or by installing pots or sculpture. Think space first. Think about the size of a space, and what size of chunks of vegetation would make a satisfactory balance beside it. Then you can decide which plants to use, and whether those already there do the trick.

Time spent thinking about what you want from a garden is always time well spent. It's not dreaming. It is how your ideas are formed. And by looking critically at the garden as it stands, and by making it provide for your needs, you will be well on the way to making a good garden.

OPPOSITE *A gardener can play with space in the vertical plane as well as the horizontal. Here a sunken area is not hidden or avoided, but made conspicuous and exciting. The same rectangular motif is drawn upwards through the panelled glass wall.*

LEFT *This path is made as visually commanding as the space to which it leads. It is still very linear and forward-pointing, but it slows your pace right down. Extending the pattern into the space on the right slows it down even more.*

light

For humans and animals, sunlight is the most uplifting thing in the world. Plants too thrive on light and air. These are their principal fuels, with a few minerals besides, while water is largely a catalyst in the process. So if we are to create a garden which is pleasing to both us and the plants we put in it, light must be considered carefully.

To make an urban garden which feels truly comfortable, it is important to treat light and shade just like any other materials, and make maximum use of them. Urban gardens often struggle to receive as much light as you might wish. If direct light is restricted to certain times of day, you must plant accordingly with lovers of cool shade or hot midday sun, so that you have spaces and plants which look happy and attractive whatever the garden's aspect to the sun. A garden sited east of a tall house will get morning sun and pass into shadow after midday. A garden which lies west of a house will get evening sun instead. A south-facing garden will get the maximum light available, and a north-facing garden will spend most of the day and most of the year out of direct sun.

Light and the angle at which it falls are part of the dynamic of a garden. A west-facing house, for example, is a blank page upon which the setting sun can draw the moving shadows of trees or bamboos or vines. A garden warmed by the last rays of a setting sun calls out for night-scented plants like honeysuckle and cestrum. Light affects how you use and plan a garden. If your garden gets morning sun only, but the time you really want to use it is in the evenings, what then? There is little point adopting an open, sky-embracing design as there will be no evening sun to illuminate it. It would be better to settle for a more shrouded, exotic form of sanctuary, relying on heavy foliage cover which could also perhaps be lit artificially. How about a cavern of the banana-like *Canna musifolia* and Chusan palms? Or stooled *Ailanthus* trees? Restricted light need not be a problem. It is only a problem when you plant species which dislike it.

ABOVE *Supposing you had a back garden blasted by sun, you might welcome a shady veranda such as this. Equally, if you had a gloomy garden, this pretence at shade-seeking would give you a dignified, well-defined space in which to sit.*

Heavy shade, like full sun, carries its own set of restrictions. Grass and gravel paths never look happy in deep shade, and both run to moss there. Paving is more successful, although you will have to deal with slipperiness in winter. Moss itself is gloriously calming, and is not used enough as an intentional surface. It is not hard-wearing, of course, but a moss path punctuated with stepping-stones can work beautifully. Lawns and long meadow grass are out of place in shade too, being the natural surface for more open areas. The same applies to beds of ornamental grasses, although, if you really want to, you can keep that waving, soft look by using shade-tolerant bamboos.

Most variegated foliage is naturally weak and can look positively sick in shade. It is best avoided. Purple foliages, too, their colouring evolved to filter out hard sunlight, take on sad, liverish colours in shade. But so what? There are plenty of plants which look comfortable and strong in shade. There are ferns of all sizes, hostas, hellebores, pulmonarias, polygonatums, bergenias, and dozens more. And there are plants which glitter, even in shade, such as the little, ground-covering *Galax urceolata* or *Asarum europaeum*, and the shrubby, spring-flowering *Mahonia* 'Undulata'. You may decide to emphasize the contrast between shady and sunny areas by making the shady areas damp. You might make a small pool or water feature, surrounded by ferns and flowering ivy.

Full, southerly sun brings its own problems. Pots dry out quickly. Soft foliages scorch like a pale skin. The soil becomes hot and arid, especially at the foot of a wall. And yet with all that light, and greater ambient temperature, much can be achieved. In this combination of good light and extra warmth, plants grow quickly if well watered. Exotic plants outside their regular climatic zone will flower here whereas they would never flower in the country half an hour's drive away. Residual warmth on well-lit walls helps to palliate frosts and preserve permanent plantings of doubtful hardiness. Make the most of such localized microclimates.

And glittery foliages, whether happy in sun or shade, come alive in a garden lit artificially for night use. The same is true of fountains. Lit at night, a fountain in shade can sparkle dramatically, but in a sunless, daytime position it is sad indeed.

ABOVE *Galax urceolata in its winter plumage. Doesn't it have style! In summer it is bright, glossy green.*

LEFT *Sun-loving plants, and the kind of garden they like – for example, a scree or gravel garden – will only look comfortable in full sun. Make your planting style suit your light and soil. Plants which look unhappy will not make a serene scene.*

soil

Gardens in cities are a true affirmation of life. Only look at a self-sown buddleia or a birch tree growing in a silted gutter, and you can see the power of nature to survive on next to nothing. But surviving is different from looking good. In an urban garden you have to know your soil and use it carefully to make a garden sing.

One of the first things you need to know about your soil is its pH – whether it is acidic or alkaline. Acidity or alkalinity are a part of the local discipline within which you must work. Knowing the pH will give you an idea of what kinds of plants you can grow – whether ambitions for acid-lovers like rhododendrons and camellias, for example, are realistic. If you want to grow lime-haters in pots, you will also need to find out whether your domestic water supply is acidic or alkaline. In cities it may well not be the same as the soil, so test both.

OPPOSITE *Wholly paved or roof gardens can still develop a generous planting structure, so long as you use good-sized pots or planters, pay attention to pests and diseases, and feed and water carefully.*

RIGHT *No garden is too small for a compost heap, especially a garden on tired city soil. Even a plastic bin tucked out of sight can play its small part in improving the soil and therefore the plants as it will break down kitchen waste into compost.*

In a city, of much more concern to a gardener is whether there is any significant depth of soil there in the first place. So often builders spread a thin layer of topsoil over all kinds of inhospitable horrors, slap down a layer of turf and call it a garden. Even grand nineteenth-century city terraces and squares can find themselves built over the rubble of older buildings. And towns and cities are notoriously full of criss-crossing drains, cables and conduits.

But roots will fight and push and worm their way into the tightest spaces. Pioneer plants, whose roots are naturally wiry and questing and which are accustomed to fighting for life in inhospitable conditions, will succeed the best. Genteel plants, whose fibrous roots are used to the easy, rich-soil-and-valley-bottom life, stand much less chance. You may find, in a garden where there are established trees, that most of the garden is riddled with tree roots, and if they are shallow-rooted species like lime (*Tilia*) or horse chestnut (*Aesculus*), then growing plants beneath them which want good soil and regular moisture will be difficult. Decisions will have to be made about which trees to keep, and why.

There may be problems with the roots of street trees or trees standing in a neighbour's garden. Established boundary hedges also impoverish the soil and make huge demands for moisture, so gardening right up to such a hedge may be difficult, however good the soil.

BELOW *A garden which has only a small area of soil can be decked out with "invisible" pots, especially close to the house, until it begins to have the fullness of planting associated with country gardens on rich soil.*

The soil in urban gardens can be dead too – having been parched and not given any organic matter for so long that microbial activity has all but ground to a halt. You will need to change this, and take to composting all you can, even in a small garden, to bring some organic life back to the soil and to your plants' roots. Small plastic bins are available for composting both kitchen and garden waste. Mulches will help too. Anything to kick-start an adventurous cycle of decay.

The soil quality will help you decide whether you want a lawn, or whether it is just too dry or badly drained to bother with grass. You may say the city is so dry that you must have some green lawn, to calm the soul, and that you are prepared to pay the price of watering it often. Or you may feel that the soil is so poor or shallow that it would be easier to pave over the lot and plant in containers. If these are sufficiently generous there is no need for a containerized garden to look mean. Soil-borne pests and diseases tend to be more of a problem in containerized gardens, but that is also a price which has to be paid.

ABOVE *Pots do not have to be hidden. You can make a virtue of their numbers, growing the kinds of small, low-maintenance plants which dress pots rather than plants which dominate and hide them. Be generous with your pots.*

water

Water is the giver of life and the ancient symbol of life. Water was what set apart the ancient walled Persian gardens from their desert environs – not just the presence of water, but an apparent superfluity of it, saying that life was secure, and endless. This might not be a bad philosophy for urban gardens.

Unfortunately water is not limitless. Population pressure means that water is restricted and expensive. It has to be used with care, if gardens are not to get a bad name as an unsustainable indulgence in times of water scarcity. That is not to say that today we should forget water in gardens, but if water is to be a major element of a garden – a designed element – then it has to be efficiently planned. The results can be devastatingly beautiful. Why should a city garden not be entirely a water garden?

Even in a garden where water is not a design feature, its presence or absence is a major factor in deciding what kind of garden sanctuary you can make. High rainfall all year round will mean that you can sustain a canopy of thirsty trees as well as a lush layer of ground cover. In other climates there will be a dry period at some time, when you may have to provide water artificially. Alternatively, you will need to plant your garden with less thirsty species which can coast through a period of drought and still look good. The palette of plants

RIGHT *In places unfit for plants – dry, dark corners between walls or in shade under the eaves of a house – it is better to admit defeat and use the space differently. Could a rustic seat be the answer, or some mossy sculpture, or just paving?*

from which you choose may include varieties which are more leathery and glossier than you would use in a garden where water is ever abundant.

You will need to plan for dealing with water as it falls. Close to the foot of a wall is always a dry place, since walls create their own rain-shadow. There may be damp corners in shade where nothing but moss or low, undemanding ground covers like *Soleirolia* will grow. Make a virtue of these microclimates. Make them simple, peaceful moments in the garden, to contrast with busier places elsewhere. Put in a log seat perhaps, lapped around by a green wave of *Aspidistra elatior*, or a piece of mossy sculpture.

ABOVE *Making a lot of a little. This raised tank and bold back wall are the basis for a simple set of falling jets. Water to touch and water to listen to, water to sit by and water to grow plants in, all in one feature.*

ABOVE *Water is squeezed into the design discreetly, to provide a place for water lilies and marginal plants, but with only a small point of formal contact with paved areas. Cobbled paving would have sat more comfortably beside the pebble beach.*

Plan also for how rainwater is to be channelled away into drains. Roofs with long overhangs of the kind commonly seen in climates with high rainfall can be fitted with gutters and the water carried away efficiently. But what if you live in a climate where there are occasional sudden storms but wet weather is not a regular occurrence? Here, if you have paving below the roofline, you might want to let the water crash down onto it in a curtain, to maximize the drama, and only channel it away after it hits the ground. Delicious, but not for depressive types.

Remember that the pleasure of water is not just visual. It can be aural and tactile too. Would you enjoy the sight and sound of water crashing onto paving? Would you prefer the trickling of a spout into a tank, or the almost inaudible bubbling of a submerged jet under the surface of a pond or within a sculpture which runs with water? Would you like to have seating by water, so you can dangle a hand into the water as you sit and read? Do you like to push a finger into a lip of water flowing over a wide metal mouth, to see how it divides and converges again about your skin, to see how it moves from colourless to white and back again?

You may want to install a small swimming pool in the garden, or a spa pool. But bear in mind that these must be incorporated into the design and not fight against it. Most swimming pools are miserably utilitarian, for all their pseudo-malachite glamour, and you can do so much better with a little imagination.

Think about how you will water the garden when you need to. Is it worth running a buried water pipe to the end of the garden? Nothing is less serene than the sight of hoses snaking round lawns and paving, like saline drips, ready to save a garden from going into shock. Is it worth setting up a buried sprinkler system which will water in your absence, so that when you come home to your sanctuary after a hard day you do not need to start sousing it to keep it alive.

You may feel that the kind of water you like is the marginal kind, where water plants hint at natural wetlands. This can be suggested in a sunny urban garden by making bog garden beds with the help of impermeable liners.

LEFT *It is a brave gardener who uses water so widely that it characterizes the whole garden. But it is an effective way to use it. There are perhaps too many different hard-landscaping materials here for the garden to be as peaceful as it might.*

planting style

Plants can be the decorative element of highly architectural gardens, or both a decorative and a structural element in more naturalistic gardens. So the planting style – bold or subtle, moving or static, clipped or naturalistic – needs to be considered carefully. The smaller the garden, the more every plant must earn its keep.

BELOW *The jungle style need not be tidy. But it must be lush, and have plants which revel in the low life as well as those which rise above it on a speedily growing trunk to form a canopy.*

A jungle style of planting is effective in a garden where you want to feel yourself deep among vegetation. It is an inward-looking, secluded, low-colour style. The large foliage of jungle plants suggests low light levels under high, canopy-forming trees, where plants must mop up every bit of light, and use their large foliage to channel the drips of rain down to their roots. The scale of large, umbrella-like jungle foliage – of bananas and palms and tetrapanax, for example – makes us feel smaller, like insects down among the roots. It is an effect worth maximizing. But unless you live in a frost-free climate where the exotic jungle style can flourish all year, it may leave your garden looking very bare in winter, when trees are leafless and soft exotics are absent or under winter wraps.

LEFT *A more Mediterranean version of jungle style, with spiky* Furcraea longaeva, *mauve* Verbena bonariensis, *and the massive foliage of a stooled* Paulownia tomentosa. *It is the proximity of plants to people which is most important.*

BELOW Canna 'Striata'. *Look at the architecture and light and shade within this plant. This is the kind of plant which makes you want to be among the foliage, not at a polite distance. It has large orange flowers too.*

You can create a hardier jungle effect by cleaning up trunks of existing trees to make simple verticals, under which to plant a low "forest floor" of hardy foliage plants – ferns, bergenias, polygonatums, ivy, and phytolacca. Then, for the summer at least, you could add a more exotic touch to the planting with bedded-out alocasias, caladiums, and begonias.

In a more open garden you might still make use of large foliage, but with a more Mediterranean style, using pines, palms, phormiums, cannas, cordylines, yuccas, and all those spectacular large but less hardy succulents, such as agaves, beschornerias, and furcraeas. It is a style which makes much of glittering foliage, and of foliage silhouetted against a blue or moonlit sky.

In colder gardens the jungle effect has to be tricked out, using large-leaved hardy species such as fatsias, aralias, bamboos, and bergenias. Trees such as ailanthus and paulownia can be pruned hard to produce outsize foliage. You can even achieve a jungle of sorts with more conventional hardy garden plants, making cover by erecting pergolas on which to hang wisteria or *Vitis coignetiae* or grapes, and by making every path so narrow you must brush against high vegetation, be it only roses and delphiniums. It is the contact with the plants which counts in jungle style – the sense of being right among them.

Some people, even gardeners, make rude jokes about those who enjoy topiary, calling them control freaks or worse. It's mean. Topiary can be exuberant, satisfying, and fun. Those people misunderstand topiary. It is not just about making plants submit to anyone's will (although that is necessary). It is also about defining shapes and spaces. In a good garden where there is a lot of clipping, the spaces between the clipped shapes are just as important as the shapes themselves. The most undervalued virtue of topiary is that it can defy gravity. It is a means of creating apparently large, heavy volumes which float on a trunk. And so, at the same time as giving that sense of calm which comes from an obvious continuity of care, topiary can lighten a garden. It can lift the garden's centre of gravity by hoisting shapes off the ground and into the air, no matter whether they are spherical or cuboid shapes or organic blobs.

Because topiary can create artificial shapes, it gives a sense of movability, of its position being carefully contrived. This you can use to advantage, promoting the popularity of a central vista by flanking it with topiary pieces, or announcing a hidden doorway. Conversely, you can create shapes which appear to have a momentum of their own – spheres and simple, rounded shapes – and employ this, or a sudden halt, to emphasize the momentum of a slope or vista. Best of

OPPOSITE *Don't these two chess pieces look as if they have been stacked in the corner, rather than grown there? There is a lightness and temporariness in their physical detachment from the ground, as well as a gravity.*

RIGHT *What a conceit is this. There is apparent momentum and real physical fixedness in this spiral of box balls. The contradiction is pleasing visually and intellectually. Who says topiary is boring?*

all, however, topiary can give a garden a calming logic during the winter months, in a way that nothing else can. You can perfectly well use it in a garden where most of the summer planting is semi-wild or naturalistic, to provide an affirming contrast and an invaluable winter presence.

Also important is contrast. The essence of good planting, it is present in the miniature contrasts between adjacent flower shapes, or between slender and chubby plants, and it is also a major element in the way colour is used. But also on a larger scale, a garden needs contrast between its different sections if it is to be enriched to its full potential. A chunk of topiary or an L-shaped corner of wall will provide contrast and balance for a large bed of mixed planting. The simplicity of one makes an opportunity to employ the complexity of the other.

BELOW *Waving seedheads of grasses are admired for their informalizing effect, but individual clumps can also be used formally, as here, to provide a wallpaper-like texture over a large area.*

In a city garden where space is tight, if you want highly layered, mixed planting which will be colourful throughout a long season, you need those masses – of architecture or topiary or tree trunk – to provide the anchor and the contrast to the planting's fussiness. Complexity needs its antidote if the garden is to be peaceful.

Complex planting comes in various styles. The traditional mixed-border style will be familiar to most gardeners, and its contrivance and heavy reliance on garden varieties make sense in a design which is more formal than natural. But there are other styles of planting just as complex which you could also consider, anchored, as ever, by strong design.

You might want to use a much more naturalistic style of planting, and make borders rich in ornamental grasses. A great part of the beauty of grasses is the way they flow in the wind. Who hasn't smiled at a cornfield rippling in the sunshine, or watched the grass around a helipad tearing away in all directions, as if to escape the noise, as a helicopter takes off?

Also hugely significant is the way grasses stand in clumps, stems side by side, like cohorts of an army. Grasses provide a different feel from the prima donna manner of the single rose or the peony, to a more democratic, inclusive look. It is a less visually competitive and demanding style of planting, and softens a garden in many ways.

ABOVE *A chunky, dense, mixed planting such as this has huge contrast of texture and colour and dynamic. But without well-proportioned open spaces or architectural mass to balance it, it can become too rich and indigestible.*

But grasses alone do not make a natural look. As well as using a matrix of grasses, nature repeats and repeats the same plants. Informal repetition of plants in a border does two things. It brings a scattery, easy-going look, but it also demands a clear discipline of the gardener. The truly natural look does not let you have everything, does not let you have your cake and eat it. You must choose which plants will do well – the ones you select can be native varieties if you prefer – and then use them generously (if informally) to the exclusion of others. And if you go for a highly naturalistic style, you must be prepared to understand that nature usually has a rest in winter. Meadowy gardens, bar a few seedheads, go very quiet indeed. And that is the time when a garden which has a naturalistic planting style for its smaller plants must fall back on good structure and form and proportion if it is to remain a useful, calming space.

Gardeners whose joy is playing with plants will probably avoid a minimalist style of garden, because it offers too few opportunities for planting many different species. But it need not be entirely so. It depends whether you are by nature a rearranger or a polisher. Gardeners who enjoy perfecting the appearance of plants can get huge pleasure out of creating minimalist gardens. Topiary often figures significantly in their gardens, and to develop just the right shape over time is a painstaking pleasure for them. Achieving the right degree of branch structure on a multi-stemmed pine or amelanchier brings the same reward. It is a matter of attending to quality, rather than creating a foaming jungle.

The plants which work best in a minimalist context will be those which offer year-round interest, and have good qualities of foliage and flower and fruit and bark. They may have outstanding texture of leaf, like hairy *Hydrangea sargentiana*, or structure of leaf like the much-divided aralias, or glitteriness of leaf like pittosporums. They may be formal and symmetrical in habit, like *Cornus controversa* 'Variegata', or as random as a grove of bamboo stems. If there is a significant amount of herbaceous planting in the garden, it will need to be of a kind which disappears in winter to reveal equally interesting architectural detail, or whose dead stems stand so well that they provide another layer of interest.

BELOW *The sculptural abilities of architecture alone to define a space may be such that the role of planting is reduced merely to tying the structure to the surrounding vegetation. Some will like this and others hate it.*

part two

*the spirit of
the garden*

magic and *mystery*

Why shouldn't a garden be a sanctuary, and yet still have magic and mystery? What makes a garden serene is a single, focused style and a strong sense of place. Why not then make that style magical, mysterious – dangerous even? A sanctuary need not be tame. Altars to the gods were places of sacrifice, after all. Only make the danger latent, and make it integral to the design. Make your garden a place that is both visually calm and intellectually provocative. Make it a place where you feel your spine tingle a little.

RIGHT *The temptation of a well-made entrance. A suggested space, out of sight behind thick walls, is a fine beginning for any city garden, but especially one which sets out to be magical and mysterious. At night, with the garden lit, the air of mystery is even more enhanced.*

OPPOSITE *Good gardens can simply be beautiful, passive affairs. But they can also contain sculpture and words and ideas that actively reach out to challenge you. They can puzzle and provoke, as well as be attractive. As in life, beauty and attractiveness are two very different things.*

Every garden has two selves, its daytime self and its night-time self, and both are potentially aspects of its character. Never ignore that night-time self. Cities may almost never be properly dark – there is too much light pollution for that. But then there is so much more residual warmth in town than in the countryside. You will use an urban garden much more at night. So plan for it. Focus on that magical atmosphere day and night if that is what appeals to you.

Once, when I was a student, I went for a walk with a girlfriend around the city suburbs at 2am. We strayed into the high-hedged gardens of a convent where it was pretty inky-dark for a town, and we managed to lose physical touch with each other going through a narrow tunnel of hedge. I crossed the next open space in absolute darkness, arms forward like a cartoon sleepwalker, and suddenly found myself torso to torso with Mary Mother of God. She was cold, white, and just – just – visible in the dark. I was terrified.

It is that quality of experience which deserves to be created in a garden. The tall, white statue at the end of a simple green space, like a secret locked in a closet, can be both a strong piece of design and a strong piece of theatre. And calm into the bargain. Give the space a seat too if you like. Not a bench – a single seat. Like a confessional. Somewhere to be alone with your thoughts.

BELOW Mystery has much to do with secrecy. This "crow's-nest" seat built into the upper layer of a pergola makes full use of its sense of secrecy and separation from the world below. With a rope ladder it would be even more separate. It is somewhere to take a rug and a book as the sun goes down, somewhere you might find a caterpillar smoking dope. Part of its effect is achieved through the way, ladder apart, it could almost go unnoticed, as a tangle of stems.

But how do you make a garden as a whole magical and mysterious? Let's look at some ways of working. More than any other kind of sanctuary garden, one like this has to have significant entrances, something behind which unknown things can happen, like the doors of Bluebeard's castle. So that when a door opens, there is a delicious shock. Perhaps there will be a pink, adobe-walled room beyond, containing only one opaque-glazed high window, and one barrel cactus or boulder. Perhaps there will be nothing but water between glass or steel walls, and a floating, lily-pad island with a chair on it. Whatever the secret, the garden has to have its "locked door" by which to enter. There has to be that moment of dark in the theatre before the show starts. So make your entrances telling, and

ABOVE *If gardens are at heart just a blend of plants and spaces for people, there is no reason why you should not intensify the character of one or several of those people-spaces, as here, to make an island in the garden with its own particular atmosphere. This balcony is enclosed with a low wall and rail, and an umbrella and hanging lamps, to create an intimate space of its own. Very British colonial.*

RIGHT *Don't be afraid, in an urban garden, to employ visual tricks and contrivances to make your effects. If you can't do this in a small town garden, where can you do it? Here a mirror gives a false sense that there is a doorway in the wall, with an inviting space beyond. It also pulls light into what would otherwise be a dark space.*

OPPOSITE *Isn't this fun? The Mediterranean scene works especially well in this ancient doorway. It frames the "view" perfectly, telling you that it is unreal, like a picture on a wall, a game. Like it or not, the eye here understands depth and a view, even though the brain knows there is none. Imagine it with just a lion mask and basin, or a trellis and jasmine, and see the difference.*

maybe the exits too. Closing a door behind you gives a huge feeling, not necessarily of security, but of finality and commitment. If your entrance is at the top or bottom of steps, it will add to the sense of rooftop or dungeon.

Let things be not what they seem. Garden buildings are structures whose principles of construction are incorporated into the design. The walls are held together under the weight of the roof, whether it is Classical or Gothic. But buildings can also be a specialized form of sculpture. You can hide that constructional truth in all the abstract or figurative artwork you might choose. Tile it. Plaster it. Fill it with mirrors. Cover it in bark. Why should a garden building look like the wood or stone it is, when it could look like – gingerbread? A grotto? A gypsy caravan? A gargantuan head, with a mouth for a door? Let your imagination get to work.

Seats can be treated the same way. The smaller the garden, the more significant a piece of architecture is the seating. So in a garden of magic and

mystery it is crazy to throw away the atmosphere with seating which screams "major multiple". Find seating which suits the atmosphere. It might be logs on end, or ancient rattan loungers, or a seat in the shape of a weaver bird's nest hung from a tree and stuffed with sheepskins.

Gardens of magic and mystery are not necessarily shut away, enclosed spaces. You can make just as appealing and mysterious an environment in an open garden. In this case simplicity is the key. You might develop a garden with an open centre using only green plants of bold foliage and texture – billowing bamboos and fatsias, and mounds of clipped evergreens, set off by a plain lawn. Against this accommodating, all-seasons background there is the opportunity to play all kinds of structural games. A modern summerhouse of wood and steel perhaps, painted in bright primary colours. Pale stone sculpture incorporated into the planting or used to give momentum and direction to the space itself, drawing the eye around the garden as you wish.

In an open garden you might want to make the ground itself the focus of the magic. Surrounded by simple screen walls or hedges, you could play with mounded-turf spirals, or make a green turf maze or chessboard, to put an element of intellectual puzzle into the garden. You can play with inscriptions too – words or symbols which can be followed through in a meaningful sequence and will give the garden as a whole its own particular associations and logic.

Concentrating on green plants is one way of making a calm, specialized atmosphere in which to set artwork. But you can use other foliage colours. I once saw a Japanese-style back garden in which the predominant foliage colour (there was little flower power) was purple. Horrible? Curiously, no. There were dominant purple Norway maples, and cotinus and hazel, and pittosporum and berberis. But care had been taken to avoid the development of large areas of shade. Light came down between everything and onto the ground below, which was grassy, with boulders, and rills snaking into mossy corners, like a sort of serene Crazy Golf course. The effect was to make green the highlight colour whereas usually it is the background colour, and the eye was miraculously drawn to the ground and its simple contours. The predominantly purple canopy of the garden floated above all this, a slightly artificial-looking layer of insulation between the landscape below and the real world beyond. It was clever.

Feel free to exploit modern materials for their magic and mystery. Glass and steel may not suit your house, and you may need to separate their world from that of the house. But do it, if you think it is a game you want to play.

And remember lighting. You can buy thousands of candles and torches for the price of installing sophisticated outdoor lighting. If you do go for electricity, use it creatively, to supply movement and light. I once ate outdoors in a country garden where, as darkness fell and liqueurs appeared, in the yew tunnel across the lawn leading down to a pond, a glitterball began to revolve slowly, throwing handfuls of light into the night, like confetti. Such magic is unforgettable.

OPPOSITE *It is fine to make installations in a garden which challenge and provoke and delight, but they must always have the kind of poise and balance which will produce a garden and a space which is calm and satisfactory. Art can suggest chaos, but should never be chaotic. Design is always a discipline, working with mass and line and proportion.*

magic and mystery

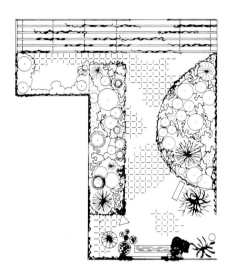

There can be no exact prescription for what makes a garden magical and mysterious. People's ideas vary so much. But aiming for the unexpected is a good place to start. This San Francisco roof garden by John Wheatman has plenty of surprises. The underlying design is simple enough. Sliding doors look out from the house under a wooden loggia, down a long, rectangular, level space to a seat and an architectural feature, in this case a panel of stained glass.

Much effort has gone into making this garden seem part of the house. Plants or architecture effectively create walls, to a height equivalent to a room indoors. A moulded architrave over the glass wall suggests interior decoration. The floor is paved in corner-to-corner squares to suggest a conservatory or winter garden floor. There is that odd mixture of indoor and outdoor plants seen in display houses and conservatories – ferns, clivias, busy lizzies, Japanese maples and climbers.

ABOVE *Note in the original designer's plan how the planting is restricted to two main beds for convenience. But it can be complicated and decorated just as much as you like with the use of pots.*

RIGHT *The ultimate trick with mirrors – water apparently pouring out of nowhere through the face of a mask suspended in space. Notice how the mirror extends both the garden and the loggia.*

Stained glass was a common feature of nineteenth-century conservatories, and here it is given a bold, modern revival. Used as a panel this way, like a grand doorway, it suggests another room beyond, yet there might be only space above the street. How do you decide when you can't see beyond? Imagine this panel glowing briefly under the direct rays of a rising or setting sun. Imagine sitting out there having dinner or breakfast in a beam of coloured sunlight. It could also be backlit for night-time effect. Plants are allowed to grow across the glass so that the panel does not dominate the garden at all times, but its simple frame is kept clear of climbers to establish its presence. The loggia against the house is light in structure and lightly but continuously planted, to provide a leafy roof to the view from indoors as well as shade in the house.

To give a further sense of uncertainty or unreality, mirrors are used. Mirrors are most effective when set within some kind of frame, whether it is within walls or a window frame or doorway, so that there is a sense of a real opening into the imaginary reflected space. They also make the space they contain seem much bigger, by projecting what they show – trees, a loggia, or paving – out into space in a continuing vista. When positioned to reflect planting which has depth and open space, they can give the impression that the garden goes on for ever.

ABOVE AND BELOW *No garden is too small to have its hidden corners. Where does this one really end? Perhaps you could surround a whole garden with puzzling doorways, instead of a fence.*

magic and mystery 53

the natural approach

Some gardeners live in town under sufferance, because their hearts are in the country. Perhaps your idea of heaven is a picture-book thatched cottage, or a water meadow with cattle grazing, or an alpine meadow full of flowers. There is no reason at all why a garden of any of these flavours should not be produced in a city, but it can't be done by trying to accurately recreate the real thing. Rural gardens are, after all, a symptom of their surroundings, just as town gardens are. You have to select those things about the rural style which are essential to it, and which matter most to you, and then use them sympathetically to make a peaceful garden.

OPPOSITE The mixed, meadowy, wild-flower look has so much appeal for gardeners stuck in the city. But it is not an easy trick to pull off. It requires careful management at all times of year, and you must be prepared for it to look less than glamorous at times. Also it needs a strong design, to carry this kind of planting whose drama is on such a small, scattery scale.

Consider the differences between a town garden and a country garden. In the country there is a liberating abundance of space, not necessarily in the garden itself but at least adjoining it, in farmland and forest. Country gardens are the sharp, high-maintenance end of that cultivated continuum of land – forest, farm, garden – rather than a complete contrast to their surroundings. For some country dwellers it is quite calming enough to have space and farming or forestry around. They do not feel the urge to have highly stylized, high-maintenance gardening on any scale around their houses, however much they may enjoy physical gardening. After all, ornamental gardening is work for its own sake, a delightful, valuable luxury, but not vital. By contrast in a town, where surroundings are hard and fixed, a garden is a complete contrast and a far greater luxury, whether or not you enjoy the maintenance of it. In town there is no green alternative except for an occasional park if you are lucky.

Part of the appeal of country gardens is the sense of continuing time, in which gardens can develop at their own speed. Everything is slower and more relaxed in the country. Things happen on a longer time scale. Walls will become crumblier before they are repaired. Grass will be longer and rougher before the need is felt to cut it. Trees will be less pruned and formalized. Nature will be much more in charge than in an urban garden.

This looks like less responsibility, although the truth is that whatever garden style you choose, the onus for keeping it looking good in that style mostly falls on you. There are no soft options in gardening – only ones that demand less hard work, or ones in which less frequent intervention is called for. There are many ways to transfer this natural approach to gardening into an urban sanctuary. You may simply want a traditional country garden of trees, lawns, beds and borders, where you can play at colourful flower gardening till the cows come home, as opposed to creating anything wilder or more naturalistic.

RIGHT *How this pavilion's roof calms down and relaxes a traditionally planted and busily paved garden, when seen from the house. It is invisible when you are in the garden, but from indoors it gives a sense of open space, through its use of a starved, lean, tundra planting, which actually looks realistic and probable on a roof. The scatteriness of the planting adds greatly to the tundra effect.*

The country garden style is one of those moderately fussy, have-your-cake-and-eat-it styles, in which gardens contain a little bit of everything. It allows the plantsman to indulge his need to try ever more new plants. But aim for lushness in your planting. Hide straight lines and edges (or the greater part of them) with planting that overflows.

Look to retain old trees, even though they may give you problems of root competition and drought. The sense of old age and timelessness they bring can't be bought. They are the visual expression of that important rural sense of time passing slowly, of there being sufficient time and space for things to develop to a great age. Agedness is a luxury not to be thrown away. Try to plant enough trees to hide nearby buildings, or better still, enough to produce a view of your trees leading off into the trees of other gardens, to make a borrowed landscape and sense of adjoining woodland.

Part of the countryside's appeal is that it is productive. It is a symbol of the good earth providing for us, in response to our own hard work. Isn't part of the idyll of that thatched cottage its apple and quince trees, providing temptation and innocence combined? And isn't the idea of fruit trees just as appealing when you imagine the fruits lying golden upon the ground with the autumn leaves? Which really suggests that, to give the flavour of a country

ABOVE *Everyone longs to walk through open spaces and wild-flower meadows. Here a matrix of discreet paving is interplanted with a mixture of annuals to create that sense of star-spangled veld. Such highly managed temporary effects can be easier to achieve than a long-term planting of flowers co-existing with turf. If you want to make such naturalistic, formless plantings, always think first how you will define them, contain them, and make them work within the overall design of the garden.*

ABOVE *Compare this highly contrived but still naturalistic woodland-floor planting with that shown on the opposite page. Here massive stone footprints interspersed with moss make a charming route through the trees. It is a clever suggestion of a natural glade. The tulips are anything but natural, but their generous and scattery clumps are as quiet and gentle as the moss, and echo the pattern of the paving.*

garden, fruit trees ought to play a part, even if they are only trained on a wall. It is the generosity of the fruit tree which matters, its honest return to the gardener, and the feeling of goodness coming from the soil.

So use productive plants if you can, whether they are hardy apples, or tender oranges, or vines hanging from a pergola. Fruiting trees involve work, of course – proper training and pruning – to establish productive forms. But the visual returns are enormous and, even if you never pick the fruit, you will be investing in that continuum of husbandry which so shapes our image of the countryside. After initial training to establish the expected habit, you can always let the trees grow largely unchecked if you prefer. The quality of fruit may be poor, but the value of a fruiting tree is not always in the quality of its fruit.

You may want to have a vegetable garden too, in the ground or in pots, or woven into more ornamental plantings in the manner of a potager. It doesn't matter which. It is the visible return from nature which counts.

Try to use natural materials for the hard landscaping of your country-style garden. Not only do they lend a rural flavour, but they decay so much more attractively. If you use these, you can have that sense of things looking gently shabby not out of neglect but because there are better things to do. Make sure they are local natural materials too. Every town was country once, and you should find out what materials are used in the older buildings – flint, brick, stone, slate? – and use them. And let plants grow into your walls and paving cracks. Let nature have its hand sufficiently to say – maybe at first glance – that the gardener is not in charge here but nature.

Some gardeners are not content with the country garden look and want a wilder, more naturalistic, and, increasingly, a more ecologically sustainable form of gardening. It makes sense in a world where nature has moved from being a perceived threat to long life, to something alive and of benefit to us, which we must maintain in vigorous health.

But wildness in the sense of undisturbed, species-rich vegetation is tricky to achieve in a town garden where a herd of large mammals – us, that is – has taken up residence. A family of deer would probably wreak every bit as much destruction, even though they would stop short of using pesticides. So there is no point gardening from a position of guilt. What needs to be done is to garden

BELOW *This artificial woodland reproduces the natural look by using only wild plants, mostly cow parsley and birch, and a path surface and route which could have been made only by passing feet. The relatively formal placing and clean, straight stems of the birches are softened by the woodland floor planting, and the log pile does wonders to suggest working, rural woodland.*

still with as much sense of design and space-management as ever we had, but with a far greater sense of awareness of the environment and native species. It must be the local environment too, not some idealized Environment. Gardens can only pay a debt to their locality. It is the locality as a whole, improved by its gardens, which must pay the greater debt to the global environment.

So what can you do? Well, there are several kinds of wildness which can be drawn from, in order to develop your garden style. The most common are woodland style, meadow style, and scree. Let's look at woodland first.

If you like the wild look, you have to learn not to be ashamed of ordinariness here and there in your garden. You have to enjoy ordinariness for the relief it is, and use it as a contrast to busier areas. Woodland floors are almost always green-and-brown affairs, but none the worse for that. A woodland floor's high time is spring, before the leaves come on the trees, and there is light for bulbs and small woodland flowers to bloom. Thereafter it will be greener and drier.

But what you have through the summer under the tree canopy is structure, of trunks and branches, of straight or curving stems meeting the horizontal in a powerful right angle. This is what you must make the most of. It takes surprisingly few trees planted closely enough to make the feeling of a woodland path weaving off among the trunks. Certainly in the foreground at least, you will want those trees to be deciduous, so the light can slice among the trunks in winter and spring, and to give you autumn colour. Evergreen trees at the back will darken the gloom and suggest a deeper woodland, even though they will not particularly enjoy being partly shaded. You may want to plant a mixture of single- and multi-stemmed trees to give the feeling of a less managed or even grazed environment, in which case you should avoid symmetry like the plague.

ABOVE *The more natural and unpretentious the garden, the more formal seating provides a conspicuous contrast. An old kitchen chair pulled outside for an hour looks far easier and more natural than a teak garden chair. So would a log on end or a couple of fish boxes.*

RIGHT *The reason a hammock looks so comfortable in a naturalistic garden is that it moves – it is not a rigid fixture. And it suggests lying down, perhaps sleeping, more than the talking or eating which happens in chairs. Everything about it is low-key, informal, and temporary.*

The suggestion of a path going into woodland is the promise of a journey into the dark, and makes the environs of the house itself seem safer than ever.

Remember that the best bit of any woodland journey is a glade, because it's a place to stop and watch your back, a place to be safer in, and therefore the most suitable woodland moment to recreate in a garden. Deep woodland on its own is a threatening environment, a tunnel to be journeyed through until you reach the light again. A glade also gives you a more open kind of woodland floor to play with. You might want to develop a glade of woodland-edge meadow grass and wild flowers, or, in deeper shade, a moss garden.

Now let's look at wild meadows. Whether lowland or alpine, a flowery meadow's appeal is universal. But remember, a meadow is managed grassland, not a wilderness. Over generations, regular management produces a reliable if not self-sustaining mixture of wild flowers and grasses which can take your breath away with its beauty. Grasslands are a symptom of open space and full light, and in a garden the suggestion of such features works best in a space which is open, not overhung by trees, and where there is good light for most of the day. Roof gardens are a good example. Openness to winds is helpful too, as it encourages the grasses to exercise as they sway and to develop strong, stocky, self-supporting stems. Sloping town gardens facing the sea can often take advantage of this, allowing you to make a good seaside meadow garden.

ABOVE *There is no reason why a natural style of planting should not be combined with modern materials and modern living. In this roof garden, a hummocky, Mediterranean style of planting gives enough form to complement the bold, built shapes, but it also has conspicuous, self-seeding elements, such as the teasel, to suggest a natural dynamic to the planting. The strong lines of multi-stemmed native trees in the planters also help to complement the built elements.*

The place to put meadow grass is where it is safe from trampling. It is so vulnerable to feet in a small garden that you must use it only where it is not at risk. That might be as a transition from lawn to the space under trees. Or you might use it formally in the open, as rectangular islands in a grid of close-mown paths.

You may say that creating pockets of native wild-flower grassland in an urban garden is too much effort for its return, especially over the whole year. And you may decide that instead you will draw upon the style of a natural grassland to make a garden with a mixture of garden plants and natives, or even solely of garden plants. In a small space it is certainly visually better value for effort.

You must then decide what constitutes a natural planting style. It will vary according to whether you want to suggest waist-high, waving meadow or short, tussocky downland. You may wish to work in larger, open areas suggesting meadow, or work simply in traditional deep borders. But whichever you choose, it will mean doing without the traditional juxtaposed blocks of single plants. Adopt instead a looser, more haphazard style of planting, but still with a generous number of plants repeated, to produce the impression of a self-seeding and self-sustaining community.

It will also mean planting sufficient ornamental grasses into your mixture so that your plantings are influenced by wind in the same way that a meadow is, so they can wave and move, and demonstrate the life of the garden and locality through their movement. The use of named selections of ornamental grasses chosen for strength and flower quality will further the chances of your meadow effect lasting well into the autumn and winter, as the best grasses die attractively and offer a good off-season effect. This standing of winter stalks is another aspect of the countryside which speaks in a garden, implying that there are other things more important than madly tidying up for the winter. And again it shows the steady passage of time, through plants. Perhaps more importantly, it shows how you as a gardener handle time.

You may feel you want a planting style altogether firmer than this grass-enriched version of a bed of tall perennials. Such an effect can be found in the kind of community of low shrubs and tussock grasses which is often found in the wild on poor, dry soils. The combination of tough, Mediterranean shrubs and grasses makes for an even more permanent effect over the year, and for a planting style with no major off-season.

The third area of wild gardening which appeals to many gardeners is the scree or rock garden. When soils are thin enough over rock, natural vegetation moves towards this style, with scattered cushion plants and occasional colonies of rosette-forming plants like verbascums which produce tall, flowering spikes. Like the meadow style, it looks most comfortable in an open garden, and the kinds of plants which suit it will be most at home there too.

A scree or gravel garden is an opportunity to do away with lawn altogether. But if you do, consider with what you will replace it. Gravel alone can be an

OPPOSITE *In this roof garden a country orchard manner is attempted. Note the simple wooden fencing separating the seating area from the long grass, and the mown path through the meadow. Framed by buildings and roofs, the meadow is conspicuously just a homage to the real thing. Yet from indoors it provides a fringe of naturalness which pleases and softens the prospect.*

uncomfortable, shifting surface, fine for plants and good for gardening. But the garden we are proposing is also a sanctuary, and you would surely want to have in addition generous paved areas, either of stone or decking, to offer a calmer, more fixed centre of gravity.

Gravel and water are shifting bedfellows too, unsettled and unsettling, and are better not pushed together. Although you find pebbles and fine gravels in watercourses, nevertheless the power of water over gravels is enough to make for uncertainty. In a river bed that doesn't matter. In a small garden it does.

The larger the stones you use in a garden, the more you move from this sense of shifting gravel until you reach the stillness of heavy boulders. The last stage in the development of plants on a boulder scree is a canopy of trees, and this is an effect on which you can draw splendidly in an urban garden. Imagine, in a wet climate, a grove of closely planted trees with the ground beneath them covered with mossy boulders and the occasional fern or tree fern. It would look wonderfully wild and slippery, and yet on such a strong framework you could play games with lighting or simple sculpture to your heart's content.

The wilder and more rural the garden is intended to be, the less opportunity there is to use conspicuously modern materials. You can use natural materials in modern ways, of course. That is different. It is a continuance of the country

LEFT *Some city gardeners long for the traditional country style of gardening, of fine lawns, rich perennial borders, and roses round the door. The lawn you can do, and the entrances and exits, but the sense of open space has to be tricked out, by hiding boundaries and suggesting a continuity of space where none exists.*

BELOW *Nothing makes a garden look natural so much as letting a plant which has found its niche have its head. Here, in this damp, shady corner, nothing but crevice plants would grow, and the Soleirolia has made itself thoroughly at home.*

garden tradition. But to add conspicuously modern materials such as steel and glass and plastic, whose beauty is their shiny newness, is to lose the point that wild gardens need materials which can decay attractively and thereby show the passage of time. The watchword here is simplicity. Use wood and local stones. What more do you need? Why introduce metal seating when wood will do?

The same argument holds good for pots and containers. Keep them simple and unaffected. Which is not to say that they can't be beautifully designed and elegantly displayed. But by keeping to clay pots, or even plastic-lined wooden or basket-work containers, you are staying within the rural tradition. If wild is the look you want, then avoid galvanized designer containers and high-glaze Chinese pots. Choose work which could have been made by simple rural craftsmen. Let your garden artefacts and hard landscaping be like nature's planting: make generous use of a few different things instead of trying to have everything from all over the world. Local is almost always best in the wild garden.

the natural approach

BELOW The path curves out of sight self-effacingly, its edges hidden in the planting, like an animal track winding through long grass. The fence has been cleverly angled in short sections, to run with the sense of slope and to avoid any suggestion of a levelling, horizontal hand upon the scene.

This small town garden, designed by Julie Toll, draws its lessons very clearly from the countryside. In the countryside, where the green landscape is dominant, every building provides much more contrast with its surroundings than in a city. This garden works on exactly that principle. The whole garden is dominated by the plain, straight lines of the wooden building, which is made even more dominant by being sited at the top of a slope. The rest of the garden deliberately avoids straight lines except where the presence of people requires them, in steps and a fence. Paths lead inevitably to the commanding building.

Look at the way the designer has handled the view from the garden. Much of it is blocked by the building, and the rest is screened by a light planting of trees and fencing. The building is as solid as you would expect. The trees filter the view beyond, suggesting that green space may continue, when in fact what may lie beyond is houses and other gardens. Filtering like this is much less restrictive, more rural, than a solid fence which turns the view back upon itself.

The trees are cleverly chosen. They are not exotic garden varieties with colourful flowers and tall, clean stems. Nor are they wild forest species. They are wild species associated with scrubland – birch and alder – and specimens have been chosen with their lower branches intact, as if they had grown here as seedlings rather than been planted out from nursery rows. They will provide some yellow autumn colour, and catkins in spring, but they are not showy trees which scream "Garden!". Also they are far more closely planted than specimen trees would be, as if they had developed as a natural community of seedlings. They suggest nature has the upper hand in the planning of the scene.

Sitting-out space is restricted to one simple terrace and a chair. There are no awnings, no plastic, nothing but natural materials. The planting at ground level is also simple. Unpretentious garden perennials and wild flowers are used in an all-over matrix planting, in meadow style. Highlights come as much from form – the spire-like yellow verbascums – as from colour, although, in a hint of cottagey formality, splashes of yellow have been set to line the path at regular intervals.

A bark path keeps the real and apparent maintenance to an absolute minimum. This is not a garden where lawn mowers roar every Saturday afternoon. It is deliberately wide enough for just one person – the one person who sits in the one chair perhaps – so that the general impression is of solitude rather than society. No aluminium café tables here, thank you. The curve of the path also serves to stop itself becoming a vista to the building. It wiggles its way along among the flowers, which are the focus along the way, until it reaches the steps. This is a gardener's garden, where you could experiment with the planting mix.

ABOVE *Look hard at this building (see top left of the designer's plan below). It may be rustic, but it is also ruthlessly linear, to contrast with the natural style of planting. Even its boards run in straight lines. It has no windows on this side, and makes no concession to prettiness. It looks black in there, and does not suggest a space for people. It has all the attributes of a working building.*

the gardener's
garden

How often have you heard a gardener say, "Hi. My name is Stephen. I am a zone 9. I am a plantaholic. I crave new plants. My idea of heaven is just being among plants, working with them, getting to know them and handling them. I have to have new plants."? It's the subjective approach to gardening, as when a poet stacks up beautiful words instead of structuring his poetry, and it is a perfectly valid way of gardening. Up to a point it provides the gardener with the antidote to urban life which he or she is seeking in a sanctuary garden. But to have the best of both worlds, to be a serene space as well as one bursting with different plants, a garden has to be carefully planned and designed.

RIGHT *If you have a passion for specimen grasses, you can make up for similarities of leaf shape by focusing on contrasts of colour and habit – green or coloured, erect or drooping – and exaggerate it by using pots.*

OPPOSITE *Collections of plants whose differences are minute are best brought together in an architectural context. The flowers of these auriculas are beautiful, but they have little garden impact alone or en masse. They need architectural help such as this stepped "auricula theatre".*

Asylum or sanctuary, that's the question. A garden which is forever having new plants added to it is a bit like New York in the early twentieth century – full of new people from all over the world, busy, exhilarating, and after a while totally exhausting, so that you have to cry, "Whoa! Give me some peace!"

Now, every gardener adds new plants to his garden. That's part of the fun of having a garden. But additions mustn't be indiscriminate. You have to lose something to make space for the new. You have to have an immigration policy. But some gardeners, the plantaholics, welcome everything. They want to try everything. And to make, on that basis, a garden or a civilization which is also peaceful is hard. Especially in a small space. Other gardeners have a more selective immigration policy. They welcome plants from only certain genera,

RIGHT *The powerful, geometric strength of beds like these can be a satisfactory foil for either single-block planting, as with this cosmos, or mixed plantings. A less robust containment of the beds might not be a strong enough balance for mixed planting, and could result in a muddled, restless appearance.*

which they then collect avidly. Or they may concentrate on plants from New Zealand only, or the Mediterranean. Or they may have developed their own eclectic style of planting, collecting varieties from all over the world which marry well with their favoured planting style. They may be gardeners who indulge in none of this serious collecting. They may simply be people who love working with plants – pruning, and dividing, and tying up – until they find themselves unable to move in the garden for divisions of the same vigorous plants. Breaking up may be hard to do, but getting rid of the divisions is even more heartbreaking for some. There is nothing wrong with any of these ways of gardening. They offer fascination and relaxation to their practitioners. But they are not necessarily enough to make a peaceful garden, something which these kinds of gardeners may also value, and which they can find through some design discipline. And once you have made a suitable layout, you can indulge yourself growing plants within it for ever more.

The point of this chapter is to show how you can find a compromise between design and plant collecting, so as to provide an opportunity for lots of new plants and still have a calm, sanctuary garden. Who knows, one day you

ABOVE *If you are a gardener who likes to play with an ever-expanding diversity of plants, it makes sense, for the sake of the garden's calm, to create strong bones. These can be walls or paving, or made of plants, or a mixture of both, as here. Within these bones you can introduce any amount of complicated planting without undermining the overall peacefulness of the garden.*

ABOVE *Miniature plants, such as sedums and sempervivums, can be throw-away lines in a garden, insignificant in a crack here or there. Or you can develop a focus for them, such as this array of clay pans, to give them prominence without losing the sense of repose. The odd mountain of pebbles will turn them into miniature landscapes with their own aura of calm.*

might suddenly find you are cured and able to say, "I am a zone 9. I *was* a plantaholic." Then you will be so pleased to have a mature, peaceful garden and not a zoo. Though they do say you can never be cured.

So, how to go about it? The first thing you can do is to corral any specific plant collections you may have into one area. They will look much stronger that way, instead of scattered about the whole garden. Make a whole bed of your hostas perhaps, punctured with a few aconitums, or a whole falling bank of *Tradescantia virginiana* cultivars. It may be that the genus you are addicted to is big – a tree perhaps, or a large perennial such as phormium – in which case you would do well to make it the basis and background for all your other planting throughout the garden. Use it so boldly that you take it for granted.

Smaller plants lend themselves easily to collections, and if they are suitable you can grow them in pots and display them vertically in organized ranks, as you might show auriculas in an "auricula theatre". But if you do this, make the most of it. Don't be half-hearted. Construct something significant – a wall or a sunken arena – which will give your collector's garden some strong architecture with which foliage can contrast. Paint it a bright colour if it would suit the garden and the flower in question. Place it where it will contribute structurally to the whole garden – at the end of a path, perhaps, or surrounding a seating area.

If you want your vertical theatre itself to be calm, keep it simple as well as strong. Think of those roofed criss-cross screens of slatted wood whose shelves are used to display potted bonsai trees. The simple dignity of the screens and the agedness of the trees combine to make something quite serene.

You can make hanging collections too, perhaps of ferns in baskets under a shady loggia, or small succulents in miniature pots arranged against a sunny pillar. Be as imaginative as you like about how you house the collection. The important point is that you marshal it together into one place, where it can make a strong, clean impact.

LEFT *No soil? Nowhere to plant? You can still be a plant collector and make an impact if you choose plants which would enjoy your climate and life in a pot. A variety of pelargoniums has been used to fill the walls of this courtyard. Not easy to water them without splashing the walls with soil, but then pelargoniums need so little.*

Another way to house a collection is to design a secret space in the garden devoted entirely to that plant. A star shape of paving and gravel, beside the path, for dwarf sedums or lavenders perhaps, or a chequerboard of paving and beds for heuchera cultivars.

If the plants you collect have sufficient structure and poise about them, you could collect them in pots to display as a group on a terrace. Buy some good pots to set them off. Not fancy, decorated ones, but a range of attractive, well-balanced pots in something simple like terracotta, so that you can add new shapes and sizes of pot to suit the new plants' habits and still maintain a sense of unity in the collection.

In the same way that the wooden architecture of an "auricula theatre" allows you to display many small diverse plants effectively, so can a strong-boned garden design allow you to indulge in a diverse and scattery style of planting around it. It is simply a matter of scale.

A good approach would be to install some strong, formal geometric planting around the open spaces of the garden, something three-dimensional and bold, which will carry the burden of a more mixed style of planting. Low, clipped hedges might work, in box or lavender, sage or euonymus, which, being

BELOW Careful choice of species allows you to employ a planting style which suggests a climate very different from the reality. Here the slightly frost-tolerant banana Musa basjoo, *hardy bamboos, and tender potted palms, along with a conspicuous lack of any formalizing paving, work together to create the jungle atmosphere enjoyed by so many gardeners today.*

evergreen, would make their presence felt throughout the year. Equally, you could make hedges of an ornamental grass such as *Stipa arundinacea* or *Hakonechloa macra* 'Aureola', or an equally erect perennial such as agapanthus. If the plants behind were to be small in stature, you could use something smaller as an edging line. Perhaps thrift (*Armeria maritima*), or in shade the variegated London pride (*Saxifraga* x *urbium*) or a small running fern like *Blechnum penna-marina*. The scale of the edging planting will depend partly on the size of the plants it has to contain, and partly on the proportions of the borders as a whole and the path itself.

The truly besotted collector might, having set up a firm edging in this way, then decorate the edging itself with an underplanting of small spring bulbs. Why not? If the edging is strong enough and simple enough, it will cope with a little overlay or two of temporary colour. You could put big drumhead alliums through that lavender hedge, or a line of camassia just behind the sage. So long as you are not destroying the line, you are not undoing the work of the edging.

You might go further and create some similarly edged small island beds, perhaps in the middle of paving, into which you could mass-plant just one

ABOVE *A garden fills itself with plants at the risk of no longer being a space for people. Open space has been retained here to balance the dense plantings beyond. And it has been done cleverly, using strong, transverse lines of paving and water. The water itself is a place to plant, as are the island bed and the little plank bridge on the right. The whole prospect is tempting rather than threatening.*

species, as if you were bedding out. The choice of plant, of course, is completely up to you, and it need not be in the least dreary or old-fashioned. How about a waving mass of *Stipa tenuissima* underplanted with white regal lilies? A block of the upright, large-seeded grass *Chasmanthium latifolium* interplanted with annuals – blue cornflowers perhaps, or creamy escholtzias? Or a group of brutalist furcraeas? Or standard gooseberry bushes on 1m (3ft) stems, or camellias or hibiscus, each with an electric down-light wired into the crown? These are all ideas waiting to be played with.

Another way of strengthening the lines of a garden would be to line paths or paved areas with plants in substantial tubs. These plants could in fact be a collection in themselves. Supposing you collected hollies, you might create a series of identical clipped shapes to line a path, in tubs or in gaps in the paving. Cutting to the same shape would bring unity to the scheme, and carry with it the variation or variegation of the holly hybrids themselves. You might do the same with a line of bamboos in large tubs, or cannas, or large-leaved hostas. It is the rhythm and regularity of the tubs' positioning which strengthens the design, more than the plants themselves.

It may be that this kind of linear structuring of a garden is the thing you most abhor. Many a collector-gardener feels like this. In which case there will be a need to create structure through more naturalistic means. To this end, think first about using dense evergreens in crucial points about the garden – where paths meet, at the end of vistas, or flanking entrances and exits – to anchor the layout of the garden and to give some solidity for your more mixed plantings to bounce off. You might like to think about clipping evergreens into natural organic shapes, which will not cry "high formality" but give just enough sense of control to make the garden seem organized rather than woolly.

Different climates will call for different approaches to this idea. In an arid climate you might achieve the same effect by using barrel cacti or cycads. In greater cold it might be dwarf conifers. The point is that you need to find natural shapes which will provide some punctuation to the running prose of mixed planting. It is punctuation which makes a garden like words – easy to read or, in some cases, intelligible at all.

Paving, like a strong edge planting, also helps to anchor a garden and give it a satisfactory logic, and it is important to be generous with the scale of paved areas. Paved space, or turf, is not wasted space. It is for you. And its role is to set off those beloved plants properly. In photographs of English gardens of the early twentieth century designed by Lutyens, the paving looks huge and expansive, despite all its careful detailing. But see those gardens today, when the edges have become softened with billowing plants, and the mass and volume of vertical plants has developed, and everything looks beautifully proportioned. There is not in fact too much paving. So be generous at the start. Think of it this way: if there's no space left for you, what's the point of a garden?

OPPOSITE *All plantings need structure if they are to have satisfactory rhythm and balance. Cacti of positively architectural habits are used here to put some substance and stability into a rockery of low, sprawling succulents. They are the shrubs and topiary of the desert community.*

Consider also the scale of paving materials. The way these are laid within a path, in line with it or across its width, will encourage or delay the sense of momentum along the path. Use this to your advantage, to widen spaces and slow the flow, or to exaggerate the momentum of a path down to a focal point. A strong headlong vista will support a great string of magical incidents of mixed planting along the way.

If you feel a large expanse of paving is too intimidating at first, think about whether it could be patterned in some way, perhaps with a grid of squares or rectangles in a similar but different coloured material, to break up its expanse and to put some proportional interest or direction into the space.

You may find your garden simply too small to indulge in bold paving or clipped formality. But even in these circumstances, you can employ bold verticals to set some stamp of order on the scene, around which you can build your medley of plants. You might find the strength in the heavy pillars of a loggia, or a series of tall oil jars set on plinths running through the main border. The object of such heavy verticals is not to distract from your mixed planting, but to give it a coat-hanger, something from which it can be hung and which will give it dignity. They will also provide a sense of structure when the planting is not at its peak.

BELOW Bold foliage planted to skirt plantings that are more mixed will anchor the whole bed and give it a satisfactory gravity, making it more calming to the eye. Yielding to the temptation to have small plants at the front of large borders does not lead to a calm garden. If only there were more plants like these hostas and petasites, with grand, low foliage.

Don't forget, in this searching for line, that there is strength in the lines of the foliage itself. The bigger the foliage, the stronger the lines. All planting worth its salt includes foliage contrast, and if you make an effort to plant some extra-large foliage, this contrast is enhanced. So if you have a pond, make sure you use some *Darmera* or *Gunnera*. Don't be afraid that these large foliages are too big for a small space. In small spaces they are even more dramatic. One plant of *Gunnera* goes a long way, of course, but who would be without it?

In gardens with some shade make the most of bergenias (including the big, hairy *Bergenia ciliata*) and aspidistras and the large-leaved species of rhododendron, such as *R. falconeri* and *R. rex*. Try the large *Persicaria polymorpha* too, and *Aralia continentalis* and *A. cachemirica*.

In tropical gardens there are all kinds of luscious foliage plants for shade. For example, caladiums have pale, luminous foliage which lights up in the twilight.

DESIGN SOLUTIONS
the gardener's garden

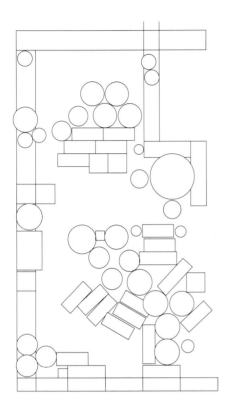

The point of a gardener's garden is to have enough space in which to grow lots of different things. There needs to be sufficient structure to carry a complex, species-rich planting and yet to keep the garden looking peaceful, rational, and attractive. This small garden by Victor Nelson pulls it off beautifully. Gardens like this enjoy the constant attention of the gardener, who maintains the physical status quo between the many jostling species. In fact they require it, since such close planting calls for constant intervention to keep it looking good. And that is the gardener's joy, snipping out a wayward twig here, feeding, cutting back soft foliage there, dead-heading and nipping off dead leaves.

This is a small garden, as the plan shows. It avoids the use of grass underfoot, opting instead for easy-care decking, which in any case looks so much more

ABOVE See on the designer's original plan how planters are used to break up the space into a serpentine corridor. If the top end is a dead-end, does this matter when you are there only to enjoy the plants?

RIGHT Among so much interweaving planting at all levels, simple, linear structure stands out clearly, whether it is achieved with planks or a fat-bellied pot, or even a fountain of strap-shaped foliage.

suitable than grass in this degree of shade and with overhanging planting, and which also feels warmer than stone or concrete paving.

The underlying design principle is to break up the rectangular space into a meandering corridor, heavily planted at eye level and at ground level, so that a jungle atmosphere is created and the underlying boundaries are hidden. But that geometry is not forgotten. Geometric planters built to match the decking, and a balustrade-style fence, peer through the planting as a constant theme, offering just enough sense of underlying structure to give the space a firm identity and stop the planting becoming amorphous.

The height of the planting in such a small space creates its own shade, and therefore foliage plants have been widely used. There are many hostas and heucheras, which will lean down and hide their pots, and ferns and clivias have been used in pots at all levels to bring large foliage into the upper canopy of planting, rather as you might see bromeliads growing in trees in a tropical garden. There are even plants in baskets hanging from other plants, and small pots clustered round the larger planters on the decking. This is a style in itself – the desire to collect plants is turned into an informal display – but it need not look so busy that peace is lost. Here, for example, where everything else is green and jungly, a white chair and a shiny table stand out as a moment of stillness, the centre of the web from which the strands of the garden emanate.

ABOVE *Just a screening of trees and foliage plants and a fence can make a separate world. Large foliage always helps to bring the focus in closer.*

BELOW *You can add plenty of detail, whether as ornament or in the form of small pots and baskets, to a garden that has an undemanding structure.*

devoted to *water*

The most damning words used to describe the urban environment today are "aridity" and "sterility". Small wonder then that some gardeners feel the need to make water a major element of their gardens, to make each one an oasis in the urban desert. A city may be built upon a commanding river, but most of the water which falls as rain is piped out of sight in foul drains under concrete and asphalt. To let clean water surface again in a garden, as a pool or a fountain, or a well, is to pay due homage once more to this vital element. By creating movement or stillness, silence or sounds with water you can truly soothe the soul.

RIGHT *If you install only a simple spout falling into water, think first about how messy you would like it to be. Do you want a discreet arc of water quietly falling into a basin with an invisible overflow? Or water which drops and dribbles and bubbles, noisily and variably, into a tank that overflows to irrigate water plants?*

OPPOSITE *There is enough shallow, barely moving water to give a sense of it being everywhere underfoot. Even some of the stone circles are full of water. There is a sense of risk, and of water to be crossed. And yet there is lots of usable dry space.*

Buildings and roads cover a huge proportion of the land in cities and towns, and climate change threatens to make whole tracts of the earth increasingly arid – a further reason for wanting to enjoy water in an urban garden.

Yet gardeners can be most ambivalent in their attitudes to water. Some do not feel a garden is complete without it. There are country gardeners who feel they have to install a pond even when the local land and climate is naturally free-draining and lacking in natural water bodies. Other gardeners do not feel this need for water, and are quite happy to garden with the more fixed elements of soil and vegetation.

In reality there is no fixed boundary between water gardening and land-based gardening. Life continues through one into the other, simply changing its forms and habits as it does so. Dry soil and birds in the trees translate gradually, through marginal plants, to water weeds and fish. It is a continuum. And perhaps this is why water gardening appeals so much to gardeners who have a naturalistic and ecological approach to their gardens.

Yet water has another role in gardens, as a purely fluid element, in contrast to the more fixed elements of planting and architecture. It can be used as a kind of moving sculpture, in fountains and rills and watercourses. You might compare

BELOW *Here almost the whole garden is wet and flowing, from stream to pool. But now the dry areas all appear insecure – floating narrow decks, or shifting pebbles. It creates the impression that water is everywhere and in control.*

it to aleatoric music, in which the composer sets the parameters within which music is made and, instead of giving fixed notes, gives only guidelines to the performers, who then interpret his or her wishes using their own feelings and abilities. That is the way a fountain works, or a wide lip of water pouring from a spout. The spout sets the rules, but the water flows and affects its surroundings as it will, according to wind and weather and light and pressure and the acoustics of the garden. It is both living sculpture and a symbol of life and renewal.

In a small urban garden the opportunity to make convincing naturalistic ponds or wetland is severely reduced, though it is not impossible. But it is in an urban context that the use of water simply as a fluid element comes into its own. An urban sanctuary is the perfect place to experiment with water.

The bravest and most ambitious of city gardeners might go all out for a garden which is principally made of water. A real water garden, in fact. To do this you would usually look to make the hard spaces of the garden into islands in an otherwise watery landscape, and to give the sense that water and dry land are complexly interwoven. There might be places for bog garden plants and

ABOVE *Take a path high over a pool and the sense of danger and depth is immediately increased. Yet still the scene is calm, and the plank bridge satisfyingly balanced on its fulcrum. This, along with the play of light and shade, is what makes the garden.*

RIGHT *Don't feel everything to do with water has to be permanent. Playing with and in water is part of its appeal. Here this rather temporary-looking plank spout offers a lovely sense of leaky wetland, and of the way water insinuates itself everywhere.*

BELOW *The way water moves and falls can be controlled until it becomes a sculpture in itself. It can even become part of a larger sculpture, as here. A massive feature such as this tank deserves a generous spout of water.*

marginals, and others for true water plants. There might be spaces which are sufficiently set apart from the water to feel secure and comfortable for sitting. There might be others in which water and sitting places are side by side, so that you can reach down and put a hand into the water. There may be bridges and stepping-stones – and risk. Hard surfaces will vary from the deliciously green and mossy to the squeaky-clean and functional.

Be aware of the water's physical relationship to the house (quite apart from such mechanical issues as dampness in walls). Water that comes close up to a house can be delicious on a summer's night or a spring breakfast time. But what about in the dead of winter, when it has not stopped raining for a week? Then it can feel as if you are taking part in some depressing play by Ibsen. So keep a strong area of paving or decking between the house and a water garden. Keep the water visibly under control. Remember, a power shower can be invigorating, but you can drown in a few inches of bath water.

Still or imperceptibly moving water has its charms. It is serene, usually darker than rippling water, and it is the kind of water in which koi carp love to slide around in silence. Still water offers better reflections than moving water, and a chance to see beneath the surface to sunken pebbles or a mosaic or a delicate pattern of tiles. It is silent.

Moving water brings noise and movement to a garden, but it makes greater demands on the design. To look satisfactory and not false, a naturalistic waterfall

LEFT *At the back of this converted wash-house, now an open-sided garden pavilion, the spilling buckets stand like a row of washerwomen, noisy, convivial, and busy. The joke is enriched by the way the buckets fill themselves invisibly from below.*

works best in a sloping garden where there is some logic to its descent, even if it is operated by a recycling pump. The greater the volume and vigour of the flow, the more you will want to see a good length of watercourse.

Cascades can be just as attractive in deep shade as in sun. Although the opportunity for marginal planting will be greater in good light, there is something rather wonderful about a gushing spout in the shade of trees and overhung with ferns and mosses.

Heavy cascades call for a deep and generous tank or watercourse below them, partly to gain the sound of the water's crash-landing, and partly to give a sense of that water coming into and staying in the garden. What is the use of a big cascade if the water disappears into a hole as soon as it lands? Be generous about what your cascade falls into. In fact, never be mean with water at all. The point of water in the garden is its wonderful ability to spread and insinuate itself luxuriously far and wide. You should match that generosity if you want to make a relaxed garden.

You can use water simply to reinforce a garden's design. A rectangular pool in the centre of an open garden will help to bring light and depth and reflection down into the centre of the space. Parallel rills running down the side of a path or a set of steps will help to accentuate the direction and momentum of either.

BELOW *This modern garden, paying homage to Japanese rockwork and water spouts, plays with the ways water sounds as it trickles through pipes, its weight and power, and the way it makes patterns on hard, dry surfaces when first it falls.*

Be careful with water levels. Make ponds and tanks so that they can be filled almost to the top. This achieves several things. First, it stops the water feature, whether a formal circular basin, a rectangular canal, or even a wild pond, from becoming a sunken feature. It maintains the sense of continuous open space over land and water. It looks generous and buoyant in itself, as if filled by rain to the brim, as if still rising; how sad and unfit for a sanctuary a leaking pond always seems. It means you can always easily dabble your fingers in the water. Inverted reflections of waterside planting meet their upright reality more sweetly and without interruption. And finally it keeps suitably hidden the workings of the water feature – the waterproofed masonry or plastic liner.

The simplest way to introduce moving water into a garden is to set up a tank with a spout issuing water into it. It can be as simple or a sophisticated as you like, the sound will always be attractive. The beauty of such a feature is that it is also functional. As well as providing another place in the garden where you can sit and relax, it is somewhere you can wash your hands or cool your face. So do not position it out of the way. Let its use be apparent and real. Style and size are irrelevant. It can be mad and Modernist, or Classically lion-faced. It is the offer of water which counts.

ABOVE *In a dry courtyard garden water looks more appropriate when it is contained in a large tank, as here. The sunken jar tells of the water's depth from a distance, and the papyrus growing in it and silhouetted against the wall speak immediately of waterside conditions. It is an easily manageable oasis in an otherwise dry garden – and somewhere to sit and dabble fingers in the water.*

DESIGN SOLUTIONS

devoted to water

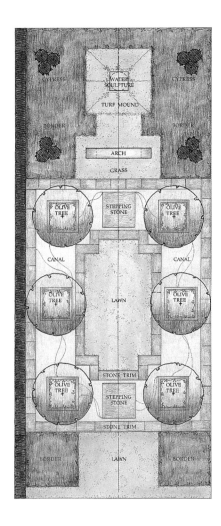

The key to making a successful garden is to be bold with the structure, and to use a restricted number of materials generously. This applies to water gardens just as much as any other kind of garden.

The success of this water garden, designed by Arabella Lennox-Boyd, lies in the generosity with which the water has been used. This design could fit into any long, hedged suburban plot behind a house. Its elements are simple enough – an island of lawn connected to its surroundings by stepping-stones, six olive trees growing in individual "islands", and an architectural focus in steel, framing a water feature beyond. But look how the design works. It manages to keep the full length of the garden visible in one long vista, yet breaks up this view along the way, so that it is not headlong or uninteresting. The steel frame effectively turns the view back upon itself, making a satisfying end to the garden, yet it still allows you to see through to the glass-and-turf water feature.

ABOVE *The designer's original plan shows the steel frame set two-thirds of the way down the garden, breaking up its length physically but not visually, tempting you with a view of what lies beyond.*

RIGHT *Look at the level of the water, brought almost up to the paving. This lets you see little structure beneath the surface (the walls and the bottom are in any case painted black), and so the islands seem to float on the water.*

Look at the proportions of the architectural elements. The steel frame is echoed in the steel rims to the "islands". The large, rectangular stepping-stones look as if they have dropped out of the steel frame, as if the whole garden unfolded from the idea of that shiny square. The stepping-stones are wide enough to give a strong sense of the vista continuing right down the garden, instead of being broken by the water. The gaps between them are minimal. Even the island of lawn, the still centre of the garden, continues the rectangular theme.

The paving which surrounds the lawn island and forms the adjoining "shores" is wide, like the steel frame itself, making the garden accessible but providing enough risk to make it exciting. Never hidden or interrupted by planting, it also makes mowing practical and gives the water a brittle edge. Shape is paramount.

And yet the planting itself is generous, even old-fashioned and cottagey, in comparison to the structure. In the foreground the paved lawn edge ceases, to encourage a soft, informal look.

The garden is flat, but is given height and depth by leaving the olive trunks clean and uncluttered, and by having water 70cm (28in) or so deep. Some designers would have made it shallow, for cheapness or safety. But this depth stretches the dimensions of the whole garden, gives a much greater sense of separation to the island, and is darker and more mysterious than shallow water. In a Bond movie it would be filled with piranha fish.

The water feature, a wet glass cube sitting on a mound, extends the garden vertically. This is not a noisy water garden. Stillness and poise are its keys. Yet the water on the cube does move, trickling discreetly and perpetually.

ABOVE TOP *See how the unfolding series of rectangles, and rectangles within rectangles, holds together a busy planting of perennials at either end. Notice also how the water widens and quietens the space.*

ABOVE *The glass cube pushes directly out of the turf, like a wet abstract volcano. There is clear upward movement, but it is very understated. Hollowness and transparency enhance the sense of motion.*

minimalist *style*

Some gardeners see a minimalist garden and say, "Where's the garden? Where are all the plants?" Others see a minimalist garden and say, "Peace at last. Serenity. Here I could live." As Mrs Patrick Campbell said, "Marriage is the result of the longing for the deep, deep peace of the double bed after the hurly-burly of the chaise-longue." But minimalism does not have to be lacking in plants. But its richness lies in its depth and quality. It is the design of outdoor space refined down to its perfect essentials. It aspires to a clarity and simplicity and transparency which can produce some of the most peaceful sanctuaries you will ever see. But beware – it will grow on you.

OPPOSITE *If gardening is about making satisfying three-dimensional spaces, then minimalism is well equipped to do it. Here a very lightly planted courtyard offers the play of light and shadow on clean walls. Look at the way the path, the same width as the door, is made to "float", like the stepping-stones, in between shallow pools. Note also how the space is very lightly "roofed" with steel to enclose the space without shutting out the light.*

Why should anyone want to reduce the brilliance and complexity of our existing garden styles? Everyone loves the fussiness of a cottage garden, or the complexity of a compartmented country garden, or the rich tapestry of a meadow garden, or the exuberant geometry of a formal parterre. Some gardeners feel that, marvellous though these styles may be, in order to move forward and find a fresh style for today's gardens, the route has to be through simplification. It has to be through refinement, especially refinement of the design.

Design is present in all those busy garden styles, of course, even the most naturalistic ones, and the most popular examples usually have the strongest, most effective underlying design. But over the past hundred years we have become used to seeing designs so heavily clad in planting that we have come to believe that the whole point of a garden design is to cover it with plants, in the Arts and Crafts manner. Minimalism declares not that plants are unwelcome, but that pure design can be as intellectually satisfying and beautiful as the most perfect of flowers, and that it should not automatically be smothered in complex planting. The way the spaces of a garden have been designed – their geometry – should speak for itself. And if space is to be given that platform to speak, it must have plenty to say. It must have meaningful proportion, and mass, and

balance, and dynamic. It must, in short, have a satisfying beauty of its own, which then can be complemented with planting.

Perhaps you can see now why minimalist style is so well suited to an urban sanctuary. Its focus is pulled back from the prolixity of species-rich planting, and it settles instead on spaces which the eye and heart can immediately read as peaceful, balanced, and well proportioned. Urban gardeners look to minimalism for a prospect which is uncluttered, calm, and calming. To go back to Mrs Patrick Campbell, this is the "deep, deep peace" of the four-square white-linen double bed, after the multi-coloured rugs and buttoning of a serpentine "chaise-longue". It is an opera by John Adams after the entire Ring Cycle.

You might think that minimalist style is something you will grow to like later, something you come to admire after a lifetime of invaluable experience on the horticultural chaise-longue. But it is not so. Minimalism appeals to the young as much as the old. The reason for this is that today everyone is bombarded by urgent, competing styles of presentation in every facet of urban life, from the things we read or drive around in, to the way we eat. Some people are happy at an early age to latch on to minimalist style, which offers sanctuary from this sensual promiscuity. It appeals to a gardener's sense of control. The urban scene

BELOW *In their way the highly stylized and symbolic gardens of Japan are just as minimalist as the most modern steel and concrete garden. Yet they are made with entirely natural materials.*

Restfulness comes from using a few materials well and meaningfully. Light and shade, and a small number of plants, play their part. But these are gardens of the mind, spaces to look at and provoke thought and calm, rather than calm spaces for people to be in.

may be a stroboscope of competing images demanding a response. But at least back home in the garden you will have imposed a sense of order and calm that can be pure therapy after a hard day's work. It will be the quiet voice of reason.

In focusing on space and its proportions, minimalist style has a natural tendency to define and outline the spaces which make up a garden. It sets out to make a virtue of its three-dimensional extent. And so a small city garden, which is by its very nature confined, can have that physical confinement – walls, fences, hard surfaces – developed and highlighted until it is turned into a virtue. The shape and proportion may be changed with secondary, inner walls or planting, but the sense of enclosure is retained. If this degree of interest in proportion and scale seems extreme, consider that is it nothing new in the history of gardening. The great Classical gardens, from Renaissance Italy to Lutyens, all used scale and proportion to give themselves dignity and a sense of rightness. In making proportion and scale matter, one is simply following in a long tradition.

Through a desire to define three-dimensional space, minimalist gardens give attention to the point of intersection between the second and third dimensions – those corners where horizontal plane meets vertical plane. These angles demonstrate the logic of a space, and the way in which the materials from which it is constructed are joined together. The way the space is made is on show, but sufficiently beautifully made as to be satisfying to see. It is not hidden with planting. And so it is not surprising to see regularly in minimalist gardens some sense of a roof above the garden, something which defines the upper limit of

ABOVE *Here is a garden owing much to the Japanese style, but much more brutal and modern, perhaps with a debt also to the gladiatorial arena. Stone is sawn rather than natural, and adversarially placed, creating an image as provocative as it is peaceful.*

BELOW *This simple moment is even more indebted to the Japanese tradition than the garden above. Look at the simple logic of its paving, wrapped around by greenery, and the poise of the two boulders.*

minimalist style 95

the space. It might be made of steel, or canvas, or it might be an overhanging tree. It is the suggestion of spatial definition that is significant.

Minimalism is not afraid to make use of large, solid volumes within the garden, as long as their proportions are good. These might be large, free-standing sculptural walls, or massive raised planters. They work as a contrast to the airier but equally well-defined spaces of the garden itself. They also provide a marvellous contrast with water. By its very fluidity and motion, water is a foil for the solid volumes of the architecture which defines the garden. It is a subjective principle set beside objective architecture, the Dionysian element alongside the Apollonian.

But water can do yet more. Still water can provide a reflective surface, in contrast to unreflecting architectural solids, pretending there is air and sky where none exists. It can bring light into a garden. It can be a surface which gives out light, in contrast to the surrounding natural materials and surfaces, which seem only to absorb it. In a heavily architectural garden, where plants may be fewer, water is ever more obviously a symbol of organic life, and this can be further accentuated by using water plants and fish. Water can be used to make sound too, to further provoke the senses in the garden.

BELOW *In minimalism, mass and volume or plants and architecture play an elevated role. Look at this striking parterre of box and gravel, so different from a woven knot garden of box. Imagine the effect of removing the paving stones. Imagine the effect of merely lifting the gravel surface up to meet the top of the stones. Minor changes have major outcomes.*

Minimalism makes much of the architectural definition and logic of a space, but the results are still the perfect foil for plants. Philosophically speaking, the marrying of human reason and nature is what gardens are all about, and in minimalism the two fit together especially clearly.

If the garden is architecturally strong, and full of clean, straight lines, then these will provide the strongest of contrasts for the curving, organic shapes of plants. These plants might be evergreens clipped to make even more geometric shapes – spheres of all sizes, or semicircles, or cubes. Or they might set out to make an even greater contrast by becoming naturalistic mounds and green clouds. But, however irregular the plants' shapes, their main significance in the garden will be achieved through their shape and line. They will be a stylized and refined version of the real shapes found in nature.

Truly natural shapes and lines also contrast well with strong, simple architecture. Perhaps the greatest and most telling contrast to earthbound architecture comes from plants which are shaped like spires. There is a contrast of dynamic as well as of shape. The walls and architecture are a fixed, rational structure, but the plants seem to soar up from the ground. Such plants also show off that point of intersection between the horizontal plane and the vertical which is so satisfying in a garden. Favourite plants showing this tendency are upright cypresses and cacti, or even more dynamic and faster-growing plants such as verbascums, eremurus, *Veronicastrum virginicum*, or young pine trees.

Tree trunks rising out of a minimalist garden are also sought after, because they demonstrate the development of natural form over time. They suggest a

ABOVE *Three principles oppose and*
find balance here – the solid
earthbound geometry of the walls,
the aspiring growth of the tree
trunks and wriggling carpet of ivy,
and the absolute poise and balance
of the round pot. Light and shade
add a changing dynamic to the whole
scene. What more do you need in a
space like this, whether it is brand
new or a Renaissance courtyard?

history and a context for the place, which rubs off on the architecture, making that too seem older and more established. Often a designer will install a multi-stemmed tree, since such trees offer a more natural, less cultivated aspect, and therefore a greater contrast still to bold architecture.

In a minimalist garden of clean walls and clean planes underfoot, tree trunks also offer the shadows they cast, as an ever-changing dancing pattern, variable as the weather, and prolonged into the night if you install lighting. It is a delightful marriage between the natural and the man-made.

Grasses have a major role to play in minimalist sanctuaries. At present they are popular in all gardens, partly because of the fashion for meadow gardening and that waving, prairie style of perennial planting. Indeed areas of soft, meadow-style planting, combining annuals, perennials, and grasses, can make a wonderful contrast in a minimalist garden.

But in such a garden grasses can have a more stylized role to play, and the grasses which do this best are not the ones that are shaped like a single sky rocket, but those which will make gentle, waving colonies of stems and seedheads when planted in generous blocks. This style of planting offers a different kind of contrast with the solid volumes of architecture. Instead of thrusting away from it, the stems hover above it like a well-ordered army, accepting their captivity on the ground. There is movement as well as order, and the effect is both wonderfully calm and calming.

There are minimalist gardeners who like to use all their plants in such a pointed, refined way that they will happily only have plants growing in pots or planters, as well as perhaps a tree or two. In pots the explosive, skyrocket shapes of some grasses are shown off to greatest advantage, and once again the intersection of horizontal and vertical is accentuated. Potted bamboos, yuccas, and palms can have the same effect, or that marvellous member of the *Restio* family, *Chondropetalum tectorum*. As a contrast to these shapes, other pots can be filled with plants of a more solid, earthbound habit.

I have spoken a good deal about minimalist gardens which have a heavy architectural focus. But it is possible to make them with a totally naturalistic

BELOW *Less sophisticated than the courtyard opposite, this space has more room for plants. These, along with their pots, play the gravity game – tumbling masses, spiking swords, and poised spheres. Focusing the planting into one hard-working area allows the floor space to flow without interruption from one end to the other, and to be just a simple screen for shadow play.*

approach. The ancient Zen gardeners of Japan made symbolic minimalist landscapes using only rock and gravel and a few green plants. The same kind of natural simplicity can be achieved in a modern Western manner, in a mossy woodland setting perhaps, or in a roof garden open to the skies.

When you set out to define a garden space as much as minimalism does, you are also able to define its atmosphere by the way you let things seem heavy or otherwise. Although a space may be defined by walls and steelwork and water, it need not be leaden and depressing. You must think about the weight of the design, just as you would think about the weight of planting in a traditional border, where you perhaps anchor it with large, simple foliage low down, but not everywhere, and create a texture of planting which lets you look through it to other parts of the garden or border. Even simple architectural gardens need this same kind of attention to the detail of their weight.

There are many ways to avoid heaviness in a minimalist garden. For a start, large three-dimensional shapes, of walls or planters, or paths, can if necessary

BELOW *Supposing your garden was merely a light-well, lit from above, between internal walls? It might be the perfect place for a minimalist garden that is a three-dimensional picture. A few plants, form, balance, and colour might be all you need. Imagine how this arrangement of shapes would change if lit from low down at night – low shadows falling across the floor and walls.*

LEFT *Transitional spaces between one part of the garden and another can often be treated minimally to great effect. What is quiet and functional during the day can become something else entirely when textures and reliefs are highlighted with electric light. Remember that even strong moonlight casts shadows.*

be made to seem to float, by separating their edges from their surroundings with plants, or surrounding them with water. Paths can then become more like rugs. Massive pots or boulders, or stone or terracotta spheres, will perch on a narrow part of their base, as if in suspended animation. They may be clustered against a wall as if having just come to a halt. Modern materials, such as steel, allow the weighty elements to be suspended, or a terrace to have a sense of containment without your having to erect a heavy wooden pergola laden with plants. Opaque glass screens create a less absolute separation between compartments of the garden, and show a silhouette of what may lie beyond. Wooden decks allow raised paths and seating areas to seem less monumental.

Any permanent seating can be built into the design, doing away with the clutter of chair legs and the problem of finding simple, good-quality modern garden furniture. There is so little of it about, and even that is expensive. Wouldn't it be crazy to dump into a well-designed minimalist garden some off-the-peg, traditional wooden bench? Permanent seating is usually the most conspicuously decorative element in any garden, because it has to beckon and welcome the sitter, and the smaller the garden, the more conspicuous it becomes. So design it into the garden. Make permanent seating a part of the space. Casual seating pulled out for summer parties will always look just that – casual and temporary – so it matters less what it looks like.

Planting too can float. As well as taking advantage of the aspiring or floating natural habits of the plants referred to above, you can create shapes which float by clipping plants on a tall stem. It can be formal and geometric, perhaps globes of holly on plaited trunks, or a colony of cylinders of yew rising out of the ground at an angle, like a formation of crystals, some on stems, most still emerging from the ground. A Giant's Causeway of greenery. Or it could be an

RIGHT *Plants with a strong architecture suit minimalist gardens well. They can create a bold effect without your needing to resort to the complications of colour and flower. They also cast more dramatic shadows on clean surfaces than a general mixture of plants. What could be crisper than the foliage of* Agave americana, *or the carefully thinned stems of bamboos? But be aware that bamboos shed dead leaves regularly and require housekeeping. Agaves never shed a thing. Just cut away the odd dead leaf.*

old box tree or phillyrea, "cloud-pruned" to look like some stylized explosion of green clouds, or bursts of smoke drifting across the sky after fireworks.

Don't think minimalism has to be colourless. There may be an emphasis on shape and form and mass and proportion, but who said you could not have bright colour, so long as it is used constructively? In Mexico or Italy it might feel very pale and clinical to have walls in shades of off-white. You might want instead to go for ochres and terracottas and the kinds of colours which are at home in that light and landscape.

Even in northern climates you can use colour boldly in a minimalist garden. As well as the natural colours of different stones and wood and steel, you can paint walls and steelwork and wood, to emphasize the spatial or material relationships between the different elements. Or you can use paint to make a contrast with natural colours in the garden – a pale-blue wall to stand behind a pale-pink cherry, or a rich-blue steel screen to define a bed of tall, golden sunflowers.

But remember that colour must work all year round in some way or other. So it is with the quality of all hard-landscaping materials. They must look good now and for ever in a minimalist garden. And so you should look either to natural materials, which age best, or to modern materials such as steel and concrete, made to the very highest specification so that their freshness remains.

LEFT *A simple terrace is enriched by small pots clustered together to make one bold pool of plants spilling out from the wall behind them. Wooden posts harden the appearance of the arrangement, already composed of plants which are succulent and firm. This is a nice way to get a large variety of small plants into a very simple space. Note that the pots are placed far enough apart to let light and shade have a marked effect within the group.*

DESIGN SOLUTIONS
minimalist style

ABOVE *Playing with ideas. The light, steel-and-glass structure of the seating area is "held down" by an inscribed stone cylinder hung from above by stainless-steel wire. This is balance without rigidity. Poetry in motion?*

Some gardeners find minimalist gardens too severe or architecturally dominated. As minimalist gardens go, this example by the designer Christopher Bradley-Hole is generous in its planting. The basic premise for the garden is a reinterpretation of the Classical loggia, composed of harmoniously proportioned spaces and inscribed with philosophical passages from Latin poetry.

The plan is straightforward. An L-shaped path is backed by a raised bed and encloses a covered seating area. It is brought to life by painstaking attention to the detail of proportions and quality of materials, and by effective and clean planting. It has no central axis or grand view out, but instead offers a constantly changing series of framed compositions within its own architectural structure. It wears its historical references lightly, a lesson which any designer working with period styles should admire.

Lightness of touch is created in many different ways. The long side of the L-shaped path is made of timber decking, which softens the architectural mass of the garden. The water feature – a water staircase descending to the path – is allowed to slide under the path (here the path surface becomes metal), further enhancing the feeling that the path is less than solid.

Seating is provided elsewhere by simple stone benches, or by modern café-style tables and chairs under a sheet-glass roof supported by steel framing. Here, on the long path, there is a wooden seat in the enclosure at the far end, and the long, low wall which supports the raised bed is deep enough and at the right height to provide seating all the way along its length. Together, the bed and its seat-wall are deeper than the wall behind them is tall, so the weight of the overall feature lies in its horizontal section. The weight is low, balanced, and comfortable. The wall, though large, has no sense of threat or imminence.

RIGHT *Note on the designer's plan the way in which the garden is divided and subdivided into proportionally related units. The dark section is the decking path with its steel bridge.*

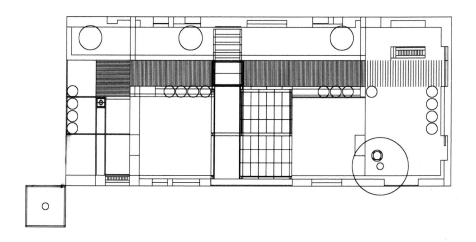

Paths vary from stone paving to decking to steel to gravel. The gravel sections allow here and in adjoining beds a style of planting which appears natural. This is generally simple and widely spaced. The busy border approach is avoided in favour of a Mediterranean scree style which blurs the distinction between path and border and further softens the architectural rigour of the design.

Mature grape vines with picturesque trunks have been brought in to establish quickly the Mediterranean atmosphere. Visually, they also lift the weight of the planting on to their trunks, as do small trees with clean stems. They also provide a source of naturally curving lines to vary and extend the play of shadows on the simple, rectilinear planes of the walls and paths. Shadow play is highly significant in this kind of minimalist garden.

Different designers might validly choose to plant such a garden in other ways, opting for clipped architectural forms, or even traditional border planting. The design is strong enough to carry all kinds of planting styles.

ABOVE *The whole focus of this internal vista leads the eye to the fragment of inscribed stone, which contrasts richly with the red polished plaster of the wall behind it. Never be afraid to use bold colours in gardens, but always use them carefully and meaningfully.*

rooms with *views*

Sometimes the smallest of gardens can become something special simply because of the view it offers. After all, if you have a commanding prospect of St Peter's Basilica or the Golden Gate Bridge, then what more do you need but a picture-frame of planting and a comfortable seat at the best vantage point? But if the garden has no view and imprisoning walls all around, and is small and unremarkable, what then? Perhaps this is the time to make the garden into another room of the house – a green room in the fresh air, but blessed with all the comforts of indoor life. When the sun shines, this outdoor sanctuary is surely where everybody will want to be.

RIGHT *A table and chairs suggests people talking or eating together. A bench suggests sitting to admire a prospect. If you want a space to feel welcoming, use the first. An umbrella gives intimacy, as well as shade if needed.*

OPPOSITE *When seen from a house, an enclosed garden needs a focal point. Here a simple but beautifully crafted bench sits at the end of the longest two rows of paving slabs, and stops the eye shooting off left round the corner, to see what is there. The slatted roof provides gentle shade and a sense of enclosure and privacy.*

How do you make a garden seem as if it is just another room in the house? The most effective way is to give it as many stylistic links as possible with the interior. Make it seem as if the inside of the house simply flows outside. You could do this by growing large house plants with exotic foliage, and by taking the theme right out into the garden, where hardier varieties of plant with similar foliage could be used in tubs or in the ground. Caladiums could nod to bananas outdoors, or monsteras to fatsias.

You could take the colours of the internal decoration and reuse them outdoors. Perhaps blue or yellow paint on indoor woodwork could reappear on a garden door or a summer house, or a terrace handrail or painted terracotta pots. You might repeat the colours or patterns of interior soft furnishings in the

RIGHT *This view into the garden would not be nearly so welcoming without the table and chairs. The bright colours smack of indoor comforts and blend happily with yellow flowers nearby to make a welcoming picture. The fanlight and glass doors also help to reduce the sense of separation between indoors and out.*

LEFT *If you have to go up or down to get to the garden, make the most of the change in levels. A spiral staircase offers a bold sense of arrival and departure, and can be fitted into a surprisingly small space. It is also rather fun to see in a garden a feature more often found indoors. Balconies and handrails like those here also offer a perfect support for climbers.*

canvas of lounging chairs or a canopy or an umbrella. You might also make dining furniture in the garden relate to the dining furniture indoors, whether in terms of colour or shape or style.

Most rooms indoors have an architectural focus. It may be a fireplace or a dining table. It can also be a picture window looking out onto the garden, in which case there will be a tendency for the focus of the room inside to become the garden's far wall. This wall needs to be carefully handled to make it function attractively, both from within the garden and from within the house.

For greatest effect you would probably make some sort of focus on the wall itself, something sculptural or an architectural decoration – even just a covered seat – which could be lit at night to make an effect then too. This focus could, of course, be a window, one which could look out onto the best part of your view beyond the garden, if there is a view. The window could be glazed with mirror glass to give a sense of depth where none exists. You could even paint a trompe-l'oeil scene where the glass should be. This area would be a good place for a table and chairs, somewhere you can eat and enjoy a view. You can fit wooden blinds if you need to close it off to provide candle-lit privacy.

The garden walls themselves will need to be related to indoors too. Plain modern interiors of high-specification wood and concrete are easily repeatable outdoors and make sense both sides of the glass if they have little decoration on them. In older houses you have to decide how to marry a fussier, softer interior with the outside. Garden walls made of the same material as the house – brick, for example – will never look wrong, but in your outdoor room you may want to dress them with climbers. You could also grow climbers on a trellis, or bamboo

BELOW *See how this garden is screened along its sides and given platform steps to take you at a slow pace – and squeezed at one point by planting – down to the end, with its bower of foliage. But why no table and chairs? It cries out for somewhere to settle down for a while – to work even.*

matting, which looks good on a fence too. You might want to raise a man-high wall or fence by some 30–60cm (1–2ft) by adding an open trellis, even if this is not planted, to increase the sense of privacy and secure, exclusive perimeters.

Seating and a table are important in making an outdoor room. A table, in particular, gives a feeling of people settling down to work, or to read, or to eat, whereas chairs on their own or a bench never look so settled. Don't hesitate to put a bowl of flowers or a pot plant on the table. There is nothing false or stagey about this. It is just to please you while you are sitting there, as flowers would be on a table indoors.

If there is an awning or waterproof roofing over part of the garden, then you can safely put out comfortable indoor furniture for the summer. This will make the garden even more inviting, as well as creating a link with indoors. But seating can be just as appealing when it is built-in and heavy. In a modern garden you might install low concrete walls which could double as seating, and set a deep concrete table beside it and another fixed bench opposite. You can make the whole thing out of heavy timbers, or if money is no object, marble or granite. By its very weight and solidity this seating will become part of the architecture of the garden, adding to its simplicity and calm.

RIGHT *This roof garden plays safe by dividing itself into an all-weather conservatory and a simple outdoor seating area with plants in pots only. Although the second is a highly efficient way of using the space, it is really just a generous arrangement of tables and chairs. The decoration and colour here will be mostly people. That may be just what you want ...*

Think hard about the floor surface of your outdoor room. A generous hard surface certainly makes a space more usable at all times. But this need not mean that it must be bleak and uninteresting. You can leave spaces for planting, and mulch them with pebbles. You can make the surface as complex or simple as you will. Best of all, you can once again marry it to the floors indoors. Nothing looks more inviting than a floor which flows continuously out into the garden, and you can achieve this effect very sensibly with ceramic tiles or wood. If door sills can be recessed too, then there will be minimal division to mark where inside and outside begin and end. The spaces will flow into each other. A rug indoors, providing interest at low level, might be echoed by a simple planting of low, shade-tolerant perennials under trees outdoors. You might want lighting to be conspicuous and decorative, as it would be indoors, and at a low level to bring exciting highlights to the textures of the planting and to create dramatic shadows. If you prefer, spend madly on lamps and candles – they will always be cheaper than any electrical installation. But if you decide to take electricity outside, the advantage is that you can have music outdoors, or a laptop.

Planting can be in beds, as in a traditional garden. But to develop the sense of cleanness associated with indoors, you might combine trees with clean trunks rising directly from the paving, putting all the more ephemeral planting in pots or containers, as with house plants. It makes work watering and repotting, and perhaps clipping, but you gain that off-the-ground, interior feel. And you can splash water about without worrying about harming surfaces as you would inside.

If your garden is small enough, you may want to roof the whole lot and make it into a conservatory. You could also, if you like that smothered feel, clothe the walls with climbers and put up an unglazed roof structure with pillars, simply to give the sense of being in a conservatory, but without the problems of watering and pest control that a conservatory brings.

In a warm city garden, you might make such a roof with plants, by buying some large tree ferns and palms and creating a living canopy. You could add a simple water feature to suggest a shady oasis, and provide some wicker or rattan furniture to match.

BELOW *Simple glamour. A well-proportioned space, with an expensive shelf for some expensive pots, and a beautiful, delicate table and chairs. But look at it at night. What a picture from indoors. It is a space meant for entertaining, uncomplicated but dressed to the highest quality. "Martini. Shaken, not stirred."*

rooms with views

BELOW *With the steps carefully lit for safety, it would be a pleasure to eat out at either end of this garden on a warm summer's night. Spaces are kept uncluttered by pots or planting for just such social use, and the indoor space flows effortlessly out and down the length of the garden.*

Here is a perfect example of a garden being used as an extension of the house. It is really quite stage-like in the way it sits there waiting to be filled with people. The designer is Michèle Osborne.

There are many tricks to be learned here. Notice the ample decking up at the level of the windows, allowing people to wander out comfortably when the windows are slid back. This upper terrace becomes part of the dining room on warm nights, and you can eat under the canopy of the tree. There is permanent outdoor seating here too, so it can easily be used at any time.

The choice of decking is a continuation of the interior, making for a smooth transition between indoors and out. Look also at the high quality of the woodwork. The sense of the garden thrusting out from the house has been exaggerated by providing an intermediate level in the decking, and the steps

LEFT *The tree has been given a discreet up-light at its foot, to turn it into a living sculpture when seen from indoors at night, at any time of year. It also tempts you to go outdoors.*

BELOW *See how in the designer's original plan little space is devoted to planting in this garden, yet it is not short of foliage. The fewer the plants, the greater the need for high-quality hard landscaping, since this will then attract all the attention.*

have been made as large as possible without making them uncomfortable to use. The decking ramp to one side likewise plays with the dynamics of the space, contrasting with the stepped main area. This would also serve as a disabled access to the bottom of the garden, where there is another large, level platform and a gazebo. Note too that decking has been used as the surface throughout the garden. There is no turf and no mowing. It is city space for adults.

Planting focuses on plants with large foliage at low level, to keep the interest and weight away from hedges and surrounding houses. Tree ferns (*Dicksonia antarctica*) are used as sheltering arms which also screen out adjacent gardens, as well as providing strong vertical substance. They are at their most luxuriant in a sheltered, moist position, and are evergreen.

The large tree near the house may be long-established or it may have been installed when mature, but the decking has been built up around it to make a void above its roots. Building up soil around a tree's base kills it most efficiently.

roof and balcony *retreats*

If the city is getting you down, rise above it. Build yourself a roof-garden retreat, an eyrie, somewhere to be king of your own castle. There is something deliciously improbable about roof gardens. They are so unnatural in the first place that they free you to be as contrived as you wish, to be as imaginative as you wish, and to play with the very idea of a garden in the sky. It is not surprising, therefore, that so many roof gardeners go for a traditional style and enjoy the sheer contradiction of it all. Their motto is not "rus in urbe", but "rus super urbe"! But, whatever you do with your roof garden, make it a peaceful space, and a sanctuary. Make it heaven on earth, but without all those choirs.

RIGHT *A roof garden is either the foreground to a view or the view itself. So planting needs to look good all year. This small balcony uses topiary in heavy pots and little more to make the simplest of gardens, always usable and always welcoming.*

OPPOSITE *Given sufficient shelter, a balcony can use surprisingly lush planting low down, with tougher plants braving the skyline. Heavy planters and heavy furniture are a necessity. Note how the tiled floor adds to the sense of solidity and security.*

ABOVE *This is clearly a space for gatherings or even games. No attempt is made to break up the open, ship-like area. Planting is minimal and the water spout and canal hug the sides. The seating is partly built-in. Sail-like canvas screens provide psychological and actual privacy, as well as movement. I see brunch parties, dancing.*

For all the excitement and risk of roof gardens, they can still be calming spaces. Of course, they must take advantage of good views, by night and by day. Who would not want to be able to see a cityscape by night? But roof gardens also need secluded spaces within them.

That seclusion can come in one of two ways. One way is to create enclosed and roofed areas where you can sit in a green environment, out of the wind, and in sun or shade as you prefer. A roof garden is intensely private, partly because it is surrounded by space in which there can be no people. Its walls are thin air, but most effective. It is this sense of open air combined with supreme privacy which makes so many people long to sunbathe nude on a roof, or to join the mile-high gardeners' club. Some even try to install a hot tub if the building is able to carry the enormous weight.

Some part of roof-garden privacy comes from having risen above the rest of the world to a place where no one and nothing else can come between you and the sun. This is significant, and it lies behind the second way of making roof-garden sanctuaries. Instead of making small enclosures you can make the garden a bowl open to the sky only. The trick is to use low seating and to surround it with as high a planting as the problems caused by exposure will allow. By this means you can create your own 360-degree horizon of greenery with nothing but sky above it. It is a magical feeling.

Roof gardens must offer real security as well as psychological security. So make sure that railings and perimeter plantings are high enough to keep you back from the edge. But vary the density of that protection, so that it does not come to seem like a prison. For example, where you want seclusion, have box planters whose contents spill down to ground level, and pots in front of the boxes too, so that a wall of greenery can be created. Elsewhere, where there is a view, you may want no planting but an open screen or railings to floor level.

All planting in a roof garden has to be heavy and secure, because of the risk of things blowing away, and for this reason large box planters are better than smaller pots, at least if they are used anywhere near the edge. Furniture too needs to be heavy or fixed.

You will find that the surface underfoot is very important in a roof garden, sandwiched as you are between it and the sky. Consider whether you want it to feel light, as it might if you were to lay wooden decking over its surface, or whether you want to maximize its sense of solidity by putting down tiles or paving. If the building can take it structurally, you may feel that a real lawn to lie

BELOW *It is surprising how many gardeners still want a cottage garden with a lawn, even though their garden is on the roof. Curiously, it works. Note how the space is kept simple – a rectangle of lawn, two borders, and a chair. But be aware that lawns on roofs make for all kinds of engineering problems, through weight and the need for drainage and irrigation.*

LEFT *Seen from indoors, even a narrow balcony dressed with a few pots and hanging baskets can provide a sense of there being at least some territory of your own out there, this side of the view. Bringing the focus closer creates an instant sense of privacy from inside. And there is just enough space to put a chair and read the paper or smoke a cigarette.*

OPPOSITE *If a view is so dominant that all sense of privacy is lost, you can create it with screening. This need not cut out the light or spoil the feeling of openness, but can simply define the internal space of the sanctuary. Modernist ornamental screens suit the style of both this garden and the buildings beyond.*

on – the ultimate improbability – would be the most wonderful luxury, and worth all the complications associated with maintenance and irrigation.

Once you have decided on your attitude to the views and the skyline and what sort of surface you want for your roof garden, you can choose any planting style which the weather conditions will permit. It might be all bamboos or grasses, or a cottage garden, or an entire vegetable garden in pots.

If you can't see your roof garden from any of your windows, one advantage is that you need not worry about planning for year-long interest. So long as it is either planted with varieties that will survive the cold, or only ever planted for enjoyment in the summer, you can forget it at times of year when it is not in use. In warmer climates you can use a roof garden all year, but the necessary continuity of planting is harder to achieve, just as in a garden on the ground.

Balconies, on the other hand, are perpetually visible, and have to work hard throughout every season. So too is your view always visible. If it is attractive, you may be happy to put out just one good chair and some flower baskets. If it is a view to hide, then you might make a canopy and screens, and train climbers through these until your sitting area is cocooned with greenery.

Whether your balcony is roofed or exposed to the weather, do have a close-boarded floor rather than a slatted one, to give a sense of solidity underfoot. You could then have French doors made that open inwards, so that the balcony becomes the last leafy outpost of the room it adjoins.

roof and balcony retreats

The secret of a good roof garden is to combine the remarkable feeling of being in a garden in the sky with enough sense of security to make it enjoyable. This garden by Iris Kaplow manages to marry the two qualities well.

The basic space is simple enough, just a plain rectangle outside picture windows, covered in decking to make it seem a less hard, and with the planking set across the width of the space to avoid emphasizing the overall narrowness.

The relationship to the surrounding space is handled in three ways. Part of it is screened with trellis, through which climbers can make a light canopy, offering physical security as well as the best sections of the view. Here you can look down on the street below. Other parts are screened by a tree and pots, which keep wind out while offering a partial and certainly a winter-time view lined up on the windows. Other parts are screened with a sculptural "hedge" of *Thuja occidentalis* columns, with a fence behind it, closing completely these sections of the view, so that again wind is blocked and intrusive views are hidden.

ABOVE *For a roof garden, always choose trees which are flexible and not too wind-resistant. An open-textured canopy, as here, is ideal. Give trees a wide, shallow container, to provide anchorage.*

RIGHT *This promontory of planting breaks up the garden into two distinct areas separated by a green chicane. (See also the plan opposite.) The pale tree against a pale sky contrasts well with the heavier green hedges.*

Planting in the pots is either architectural (the ivy pyramids) or for foliage colour (coleus and caladium), and all the planters are large and heavy enough to look secure and comfortable on a windy roof garden. The small tree, however, demonstrates the movement of the wind. There is enough tough evergreen content to give the garden a presence in winter even in such an exposed place.

The furniture is delicate so that the open space is not choked, and the sections of hedge in raised linear planters emphasize the extent of the floor area.

Maintenance in this garden is minimal – little more than watering and clipping the hedges and ivy, and seasonally replacing tender plants.

ABOVE *A solid boundary rising to eye level or just above brings the optimum sense of privacy and security. Any additional height is a luxury, and can even feel imprisoning. Here colour is provided by foliage – varieties of coleus – rather than flowers, keeping maintenance to a minimum.*

BELOW *The original design plan for the garden by Iris Kaplow.*

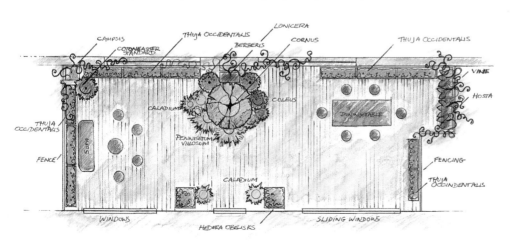

family *havens*

It is asking a great deal of a garden to expect it to satisfy the needs of a family of adults and children. Adults might want peacefulness, and space to garden creatively if they have time. Children have other preoccupations. Games. Speed. The physical pleasure of not being still. It is the unrepeatable madcap exuberance of childhood which adults miss most when their children are grown. But in the meantime, if a garden is to serve two masters, it has to be carefully planned. Then it can be a sanctuary for adults and children.

RIGHT *Children, almost more than adults, want to have space around them. Try never to break up the long lines of a garden. Instead, let the distance show. Play features, such as this sandpit and swing, can be designed and built in, so that they are substantial elements in the design, rather than looking like add-on clutter.*

OPPOSITE *Alternatively, set aside discreet spaces for play equipment, especially if you have the coloured plastic kind, which is so hard to integrate into a garden. Here a generous area of paving, together with strong, built-in seating, helps to keep a sense of spaciousness.*

To a grandparent, parked in a deckchair, children must seem like large hoverflies which suddenly shoot in a straight line from one place to another for no apparent reason. Why do they do it? There is no reason. To feel the luxurious energy of youth, if you like, which no one should deny. How then to cater to children in a city garden?

Show children a long garden or a big space and they're off, racing down to the end. That's good. It is part of learning to be confident and brave. So make the most of long distances in the garden for them. But city gardens are not often large. The best way to give children running space may be to create a circuit of paths, a loop system in a figure of eight, which they can chase around. It could be in both the horizontal and vertical planes, like an assault course – up trees, through tunnels, over bridges.

Does this sound a recipe for a mess? It need not be. It is all a matter of planning it so there is space for people and space for plants, and space for its own sake. Paths need to be wide and generous so that adjoining beds and borders are at minimal risk from flying limbs or bicycle wheels. There need to be plants along the edges which are tough and resilient, and can stand a certain amount of pushing and shoving and grabbing – indestructibles like bergenia, *Brachyglottis* 'Sunshine' and *Coreopsis verticillata*.

Along some of the minor paths there can be narrow places, which children can enjoy squeezing through, perhaps between clumps of bamboos or grasses. A tree beside a path (or in the middle of a path) might be given a rope ladder leading up into its branches, or a tree house in its crown.

It is important to link all the places where a child is expected to go with a suitable surface underfoot, so the garden does not develop that worn, tired look. In shade you will need to use paving. Gravel is cruel to fall on, and looks too shabby too soon under hard wear – unless your hobby is raking.

In sun there is the choice of grass or paving. Grass is kind to children and to adults, and softens the feel of a garden. But it will not stand the constant wear of hurricane feet in the same places hour after hour and day after day. So try to use grass in places which are not the automatic thoroughfares of a garden. If the lawn is at the centre of the garden, try to arrange that its entrances and exits are wide, so the wear is spread over a bigger area. Make the lawn finish with paving if you can, rather than a cut turf edge, so it does not get broken down by jumping feet. It will make mowing and edging easier too.

Decking is warmer than paving, and dries faster than grass after rain. But it can be slippery and it splinters, and it is noisy and can be more easily marked by dragging things around or by construction games. Don't think of it as a panacea. Concentrate on making a garden which is sufficiently paved to be clean and usable in most weathers, and then use the materials which suit you and it best.

Children need security in a garden in the same way that adults want serenity. So make sure the perimeter of the garden is physically secure, and then you can

OPPOSITE *Make the most of the vertical dimension for children. A strong tree can provide the place for a simple tree house, somewhere children can call their own, a sanctuary within a sanctuary. Make it safe but not sanitized: children love a bit of risk. If it is weatherproof, so much the better, as it will get much more use. Natural materials always fit into a garden more discreetly than man-made ones.*

relax. Avoid unnecessary internal gates and make the entrances between different compartments of the garden generously wide.

Children love racing up and down steps, but use them if you can in places where they are not part of a route where a runner might trip. Use them where they really show. Then they will be safer to play on (as they surely will be played on). Make height a virtue. If you want a play house, why not have it set up on steps 1m (3ft) off the ground, to increase the sense of adventure?

Children also love water in a garden. But whereas an adult may want simply to watch and listen, children want to be in there, feet first, fishing for newts or catching water boatmen. So if you want to have a pond, make it shallow enough to be safe, or use instead a raised tank of such a height and size that a child is not likely to fall into it.

BELOW *Children love ordinariness in a garden, simple things which they can play with without having to worry about causing damage. This kind of spiral paving is sure to appeal to children, who, remember, are so much closer to it than adults. Water is closer too, and easier to play in. And flowers are at eye and nose level.*

LEFT *Family gardens need lots of seating, places where you can plonk yourself down in comfort at any time. None-too-precious soft furnishings make a welcoming touch. It is good to have seating that is tucked away, like this, as well as the more prominent tables and chairs. Wouldn't this be the perfect place for a bedtime story?*

Children enjoy gardening too. If you want to encourage them in this, consider keeping a sunny space for some vegetable growing, and maybe set aside part of it for a children-only plot. There is nothing like ownership for developing a sense of responsibility.

Use plants too at your children's level which are aromatic – the rosemary bush on the corner, the lavender hedge by the back door. Let them learn the sensory pleasures of a garden – the smell of rosemary or lad's love – early enough and they will stay with them for life. It is important to let children see that gardening can be an art, and an absorbing one. But it is also important to put the finer gardening where it is not at risk from their games, somewhere you need not say, "Don't" but can always say, "Come and look". It is surprising how often children will join in a discussion with parents about which plant goes well with which, or why it could be fun to put those two colours together. This helps them to realize at an early age that gardening is about ideas and space making, and not just about remembering to water or how to stop things dying.

If the preoccupation of children in a garden is space, for adults it is time. We spend our gardening lives handling time, making plants come together at the right season, dealing vegetable life and death, valuing ancient tree trunks for the way they show the slow passage of time and the timescale against which our brief human lives must fit. A family garden has to combine the needs of space and time. The place to fit in the sanctuaries for adults is in the garden's side-chapels, those spaces which are culs-de-sac off the children's and everybody else's main thoroughfares. Perhaps it might be a simple hedged enclosure with a heavy table and chairs where you could

Help children to learn that gardens can be productive places as well as peaceful, ornamental spaces. Growing things to eat can be the fast track to producing a child who likes gardening. So tuck in some herbs and easy vegetables, even into ornamental plantings, if you can. If these can be started from seed, so much the better, so that the child sees the whole process through from the start.

sit and write, or a corner bed deep enough to let you play with a bold planting of shrubs and perennials and which is not in the line of any child's A-to-B.

Family gardens are not family gardens for ever. So the main social spaces of a garden still need to be well proportioned if they are to satisfy the eye and mind. Only for now the emphasis of how they are used and lived in will be different. A free-standing tree on the lawn may just now have a rope swing tied onto a strong branch, and a bark or sand pit below so the grass does not look perpetually worn. There may be a long, heavy table and benches where a family can eat together, perhaps under an awning which will cast shade from the midday sun and provide a enclosure to light with lanterns at night. It will be nothing precious or posed, but just a comfortable family place to eat or scribble.

Paved areas may have a scattering of toy tractors or outdoor chess pieces. It is wise to build some seating which doubles as a toy locker, close to where toys are used, so that you can make some clear space when it is needed. Have a shed too which is big enough for tools, all those bicycles and pet food. And if you buy swings or climbing frames, decide whether you will accept plastic-finished items in uncompromising primary colours which shout their presence 365 days a year, or you want wooden apparatus which will blend in more kindly.

As a general principle, it is always better to build seating and storage into a family garden. Children bring so much of their own clutter that the simpler the design of the garden itself, the less cluttered the whole effect will be. So build in that barbecue too, if you can. It is one less thing to kick about.

BELOW *In a large family of older children, the most important use of the garden may be as another living room – space in which to work, read, or enjoy a snack. This roof terrace is amply supplied with tables and chairs, so people can go out there at any time, and they can work separately if they need to. It's another of those spaces, dressed with some plants but requiring people to fill the prominent positions.*

family havens

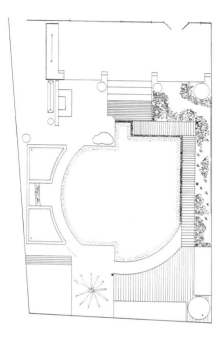

Family gardens have to combine resistance to wear and tear, from all kinds of social uses, with the ability to look good. It is not an easy trick to pull off. In this small city garden Jayne Ford has taken an interesting approach to the problem.

A wide terrace just under the walls of the house leads down steps to a central lawn surrounded by a decking path, gravelled borders, and a fence. A ruthlessly low-maintenance approach has been taken to the planting. This would not suit a keen plantsman gardener, but for a busy family it may be perfect.

The garden is surrounded by other houses and raised above them, and, in order to screen them out and provide privacy, a tall fence has been installed and painted a prominent silvery blue-grey. This colour, together with the emphasis on woods and pebbles and gravel, gives the garden a seaside flavour.

The steps are made of recycled railway sleepers sawn in half, providing a tough surface which will not be easily damaged and will require no special protection from stampeding children. To reduce wear to the grass, the apron of decking below the steps gives a wide choice of places to cross onto the lawn.

ABOVE *As the original designer's plan shows, a tall fence and a circular lawn give this rectangular garden a private, central focus. It would have been easy to fill the centre with planting, but it was kinder for children to leave it as green playing space.*

RIGHT *How much more simple and effective it is to build a large planter like this, than to have clusters of pots and a piece of sculpture between them. Maintenance is far easier too.*

Planting is restricted to bold, architectural plants such as Chusan palm
(*Trachycarpus fortunei*) and *Fatsia japonica*, and the venerable multi-stemmed
tree in the centre of it all, which, importantly, stops the garden looking brand-
new. On one side of the garden the screening provided by the fence is enhanced
by a huge raised planter filled with tall bamboos. A simple seat is built into the
centre of the planter, and backed by tall steel poles which echo the colour of
the fence and the habit of the bamboos. When they are established the bamboos
will provide an almost solid screen which nevertheless will allow a glimpse of a
view in the centre between the poles. Their main value in a simple garden like
this is that they provide movement when the rest of the planting is static.

At the far end of the garden the decking has been widened to take a table
and chairs, a barbecue, and a planter. All these are of shiny metal, and they
create clean, modern silhouettes against the fence. The fence also works as a
screen onto which shadows from the architectural planting can be cast, as
well as the shadows of the tree's foliage and branches.

The swing fastened to the tree provides a welcoming and animated aspect
to the lawn, and stops it looking empty, although care will need to be taken to
stop the turf becoming worn away beneath it.

ABOVE AND BELOW *The junction of
gravel and turf is difficult to take care
of. To make this easier, particularly if
the line is significant to the design of
garden, insert a fixed metal or wooden
lip to separate the two surfaces.*

directory of plants

This directory is not exhaustive, and every gardener will want to pursue his or her own choice of plants and style of planting. But these plants are tough, easy to grow, and, most importantly, have a long season, through either their flowers or their foliage alone. In a small city garden no space can be wasted. This list will allow you to make the bones of a garden, around which you can develop your own interests.

Z = US HARDINESS ZONE

Trees

AILANTHUS ALTISSIMA

The "tree of heaven" can make a large deciduous tree. In its early years it is dramatically fast and straight of growth. It is perfectly hardy but needs sufficient summer heat to ripen the new growth, or it may be nipped back by early frosts. Its pinnate foliage can be up to 60cm (24in) long, and cutting it back periodically produces even grander foliage. Suckering can occasionally be a problem after root damage. Where male and female trees are in reasonable proximity, orangey-red winged fruits are produced in early autumn, which look wonderful against pale stucco walls and blue skies. Z 4–8.

AMELANCHIER LAMARCKII

An excellent tree for small gardens. Drooping racemes of white flowers in spring are followed by fiery autumn foliage before the leaves drop. It can be bought as a single- or multi-stemmed tree, and it has a willingness to produce new shoots low down the trunk. Prefers moist, lime-free soils. Z 4–9.

GINKGO BILOBA

What other tree is so tolerant of pollution and (once established) drought? It is slow-growing, casts a delicate shade, and produces wonderful butter-yellow autumn colours. Young trees have a narrow, upright habit, and there are several forms suitable for street planting. You can also train it as an espalier, making a feature of the fan-shaped foliage. Choose a male clone if you can. Females, if pollinated by a nearby male, produce vile-smelling fruit. Z 4–9.

MAGNOLIA GRANDIFLORA

A marvellous round-headed evergreen tree, it can be planted in the open or trained against a wall. Large, perfumed flowers are set off marvellously by the big evergreen foliage. 'Exmouth' is a very hardy clone with long, pale foliage. 'Goliath' has more rounded, crinkled leaves. Remember this tree has shallow, hungry roots and drops its old foliage in summer. Z 8–10.

MALUS DOMESTICA & PYRUS COMMUNIS

Apples (Z 3–9) and pears (Z 2–10) bring a rural, productive feeling to a garden. As seriously cropping trees they will require regular skilled maintenance, but even as trees left simply to grow and fruit as they choose, they will still bring their own special atmosphere. The same is true of crab apples and medlars.

PINUS

The new bottle-brush foliage of pines has a simple drama which works well against clean walls and empty spaces. Older trees develop a cragginess which is also valuable, and can be brought into small gardens by using the smaller species such as *P. mugo* (Z 3–7). Pines are trees of open country, and near buildings become more prone to insect attack. So choose species which are used to the city warmth you offer – flat-headed *P. pinea* (Z 8–10) perhaps, or the feathery, slightly tender *P. montezumae* (Z 6–8).

PLATANUS X HISPANICA

The London plane is an invaluable deciduous city tree, tolerant of so much drought and pollution. It is noted for the scaly, flaking bark of older trunks, and its ability to withstand heavy pruning or pollarding. This is a tree you can work very hard, to make screens or espaliers pruned back to a framework every year. Its only drawback is that the large palmate foliage decays only very slowly. Z 4–9.

ROBINIA PSEUDOACACIA

The false acacia is a spiny tree with delicate, feathery foliage and white pea flowers in early summer. Root damage can cause suckering. In old age the trunks develop marvellously sinewy, twisted bark. *Robinia* tolerates city life well, enjoys the heat, and provides a delicate branch structure for the winter months. The yellow form 'Frisia' is much admired. Z 4–9.

TAXUS BACCATA

English yew is most shade-tolerant and will make understorey screening where little else would survive, but it also thrives in full sun. It can be clipped into the tightest of shapes or hedges. Female plants in good light will produce thousands of red, fleshy fruits. The form 'Lutea' has yellow fruits. There are golden forms

*Espalier pear (*Pyrus communis*) tree*

and variegated forms, narrow, upright forms and wide, drooping forms, and all clip well. Yellow forms must have sun. Z 5–8.

TRACHYCARPUS FORTUNEI

The Chusan palm is probably the hardiest of the palms, and has fan-shaped foliage up to 70cm (28in) across, on a single hairy, brown trunk. Young plants spend several years developing girth before the trunk begins to extend. So it is worth spending money on a plant which has some size to begin with. *T. wagnerianus* is nearly as tough. Its foliage is slightly smaller but much firmer and more glamorous. Both Z 7–11.

Evergreen shrubs

ABELIA GRANDIFLORA

A medium-sized, semi-evergreen shrub which flowers throughout the summer and autumn, even in poor, dry soil. Flowers white, with a tinge of pink and coppery calyces around. 'Frances Mason' is less vigorous, with yellow and green foliage. Full sun. Z 6–9.

ABUTILON VITIFOLIUM

An easy-come easy-go tall shrub with felted, grey-green, palmate foliage. The clusters of big mallow flowers are mauve to white. Grow it in sun or part shade. Moderately hardy. It will stand many degrees of winter frost, but is liable to bark-split and death if a late frost catches it when the sap is rising fast. Use it for fast filling of spaces and screening. Seven to eight years is a good life for this plant. Then start again with cuttings or seedlings. The hybrid *A. x suntense* is violet blue, and the foliage greener. Z 8–9.

ARBUTUS UNEDO

A bold, lime-tolerant evergreen heather, with leathery, elliptical leaves, creamy bell flowers, and round, red fruits. It can be clipped to form large shapes or screens, and regenerates well from the base if harder pruning is required. If you want your arbutus to develop into a tree, consider instead the less hardy *A. x andrachnoides*, which will eventually produce red, peeling bark. Z 8–10.

AUCUBA JAPONICA

The spotted laurel is not to be dismissed, however much it was a favourite of nineteenth-century public parks. Tough as old boots and able to thrive in deep shade among tree roots. What else will give you glossy evergreen foliage and red berries in those conditions? Care for it better and it will reward you even more. Look out for the clones with the best marked foliage, such as *A. j.* 'Crotonifolia' (female) and the compact, all-green *A. j.*'Rozannie', which has male and female flowers. Z 7–10.

AZARA

Azaras are small evergreen trees or shrubs of distinction. *A. serrata* (3-4m/10–13ft) (Z 9–10) has small leaves and produces fragrant yellow powder puffs of flower in summer. *A. microphylla* is a slender, upright tree or shrub for tucking into half shade. It has tiny, yellow, vanilla-scented winter flowers which perfume the breeze (Z 8–11).

BAMBOO

What garden is complete without a bamboo somewhere? In small city gardens, plant only the better-behaved species, because these will not run at the root and take over. Favourites include the black-stemmed *Phyllostachys nigra*, *Fargesia murieliae*, *Semiarundinaria fastuosa*, *Chusquea culeou*, and the little *Pleioblastus variegatus*. It is always better to offer a moist soil if you can, as dry soils can make even the best-behaved species quest outwards to search for more moisture. All Z 7–11.

Azara microphylla

BRACHYGLOTTIS 'SUNSHINE'

Once known as *Senecio greyi*, this is a tough, rolling, grey-leaved shrub which covers itself in yellow daisies every summer. Hard frosts may cut it to the ground, but it usually recovers. It makes excellent low hedges, or a skirt to taller shrubs. Z 9–11.

BUXUS SEMPERVIRENS

The dense habit and small foliage make box perfect for clipping. On poor, dry soils it will survive and even thrive eventually, but if you want speed of growth, feed and water it well at first. For the natural habit of box, look to some of the arching or pendulous named clones such as 'Parasol' and 'Langley Beauty'. Full sun. Z 5–8.

CAMELLIA

Camellias require an acid soil, and so in alkaline gardens they may need tub culture. In general they tolerate summer-dry town soils considerably better than rhododendrons. The glossy leaf is more attractive in summer than most run-of-the-mill hybrid rhododendrons. Full sun to part shade, depending on species and variety. Z 7–8.

CEANOTHUS

Sunny city walls are the perfect place to grow the more glamorous evergreen ceanothus such as *C. impressus* 'Puget Blue' (Z 7–11), *C. arboreus* 'Trewithen Blue', and 'Concha' (both Z 9–10). Pinch them back regularly through the summer in the first few years to establish a dense cover over the wall, but one which does not stick forward too far. Dense, well-covered plants also survive the cold better, and protect their trunks from bark-split.

CHOISYA TERNATA

In a warm corner this rich-green aromatic shrub can make a glossy mound 3m (10ft) tall, though it can be controlled at half this height. It needs full sun to flower best. Plant it where you can smell the flowers and rub the foliage as you pass. The golden form *C.t.* 'Sundance' is wonderfully cheerful if grown in full sun. *C.t.* 'Aztec Pearl' is smaller, less dense, and more delicate. Both Z 8–10.

CORDYLINE AUSTRALIS

The New Zealand cabbage tree is so much more glamorous than its name. Light-green, spiky foliage on tall single or multi-stemmed trunks, great bunches of honey-scented flowers – what more can you ask? A little more hardiness perhaps, but that is all. The purple, yellow, and variegated forms are less vigorous all round, which can be an advantage. Full sun. Z 8–10.

DICKSONIA AUSTRALIS

This hardiest of tree ferns is widely available, and will stand a touch of frost. The growing bud is at the top of the trunk, so that if it is killed the whole plant dies. It makes a fine if very thirsty tub specimen, and gives instant jungle flavour to a garden. In cooler climates grow it in full summer sun. In hotter climates you may need to offer overhead shelter. If you can overwinter it in a cool conservatory, so much the better. Z 8–10.

ELAEAGNUS

Elaeagnus x ebbingei (Z 3–8) flowers sweetly in autumn and tolerates shade remarkably well for a grey-leaved plant. E. x ebbingei 'Gilt Edge' (Z 7–11) has a paler-yellow variegation than E. pungens 'Maculata' (Z 7–9), but is more elegant and striking, if less glossy. These need full sun. None has an elegant habit, and they need pruning to keep them dense and self-contained.

EUONYMUS

Euonymus are among the toughest most adaptable of evergreens. E. fortunei (Z 4–9) and its many variegated forms will make a low hedge if clipped, or a large, loose mound, or can be allowed to climb up a wall with a little support. E. japonicus (Z 6–9) is larger, glossy, and again has variegated forms. It makes a medium-sized hedge and the straight, green form tolerates shade well.

FATSIA JAPONICA

This must be among the most dramatic of large-leaved hardy evergreens. Fat stems fan outwards, covered in glossy, fan-shaped, fingered foliage, and topped by panicles of white, globe-shaped flower clusters in autumn. It is happy in dry shade. Its hybrid with ivy, Fatshedera, is just as useful but less substantial, and has variegated forms. Z 7–10.

GARRYA ELLIPTICA

Some people think garrya boring. In summer, true, it is a drab evergreen. But in a simple courtyard where it is tightly trained onto a wall it can be smart enough. Then, when those long, grey-green catkins hang all over it in winter, all is forgiven. Dry soil and partial shade. Z 9–10.

HEBE

Hebes enjoy warm city life, though not very hardy, and flower over a long period. Generally the bigger the leaf and flower, the more tender the variety or species. They will tolerate drought well, but perform better in soils which are regularly watered. H. cupressoides 'Boughton Dome' is very different. It makes a flowerless dome 1m (3ft) across, and is deliciously aromatic in heat. Full sun. Z 8–9.

HEDERA

When cuttings are taken of the mature, flowering growth of any ivy, a bush is produced, not a climbing plant. It makes a marvellous, shade- and drought-tolerant, flowering, berrying evergreen mound, which no city garden should be without. It looks fine leaning over a raised pool or basin. The form poetarum has yellow berries which contrast well with the foliage. Z 5–9.

ILEX

The hollies are all useful in city gardens, but remember that it takes a male and a female plant to produce berries on the female. There are so many varieties to choose from – green, variegated, and spine-free. Some of the best include I. aquifolium 'J.C. van Tol' (green, spineless, female) and I.a. 'Myrtifolia' (male, narrow, miniature foliage on a dense plant, good for clipped shapes)(both Z 7–9), and I. x altaclerensis 'Hodginsii' (green, male, with broad, dark foliage and purple stems) Z 7–11. The green forms tolerate shade.

LAURUS NOBILIS

The bay tree is an accommodating evergreen, nice to have around for its culinary uses, but not the most remarkable of evergreens. It makes a large, multi-stemmed shrub or small tree, and drops a great deal of old leaf in summer. Grow it if you must. Full sun. Z 8–10.

LIGUSTRUM

Ligustrum lucidum and its variegated forms make large shrubs or small trees, with elegant, shining foliage and panicles of white autumn flowers. A grand plant tolerant of poor, dry soil (Z 8–10). The common golden privet, L. vulgare 'Aureum', is useful for providing easily clippable fast shapes (Z 5–11). L. japonicum 'Rotundifolium' slowly makes the glossiest of tight spheres, with foliage round as a penny packed tight on the bush. It is topiary without clipping (Z 6–9).

MAHONIA

Mahonias are valuable for their bold, pinnate foliage and scented yellow winter flowers. They tolerate shade and poor, dry soils remarkably well, though they flower less well in deep shade. Look out for *M. x wagneri* 'Undulata' as a glossy hedging species and *M. x media* 'Charity' for a large, fan-shaped shrub. Both Z 7–11.

OSMANTHUS DELAVAYI

A neat, medium-sized shrub with small leaves and tubular, sweetly scented flowers in spring. After flowering it can be clipped to shape. The regrowth will flower again the following spring. *O. x burkwoodii* is a larger, cruder version of the same thing. *O. heterophyllus* and its variegated forms have holly-like leaves, and clip well, but are less inclined to flower. Full sun. All Z 7–9.

PHILLYREA LATIFOLIA

A glamorous, small-leaved tree or shrub, and the richest of racing greens. It stand clipping well, and can be used for hedges, topiary, and larger shapes of all kinds. Similar to *Ilex* 'Myrtifolia'. Grow it and learn to admire it. Full sun. Z 7–9.

PHLOMIS FRUTICOSA

A medium-sized shrub with grey-green felted foliage and whorls of yellow flowers in early summer. Dense and a valuable contrast for the unusual way its flowers are borne (Z 4–8). *P. anatolica* 'Lloyd's Variety' is even more silvery but hardly flowers (Z 7–10). Full sun.

PITTOSPORUM

This race of trees and shrubs is moderately frost-hardy. *Pittosporum tenuifolium* makes a clippable shrub with small, crinkled leaves, and comes in green, purple, and variegated forms. 'Irene Paterson' is perhaps the best variegated form. 'Tom Thumb' is a dwarf purple. Useful for making shapes in cool pale colours. *P. tobira* is less hardy still and has larger glossy foliage, but its flowers are as sweet as orange blossom. Good drainage and full sun. All 9–10.

PRUNUS

This genus includes all the old ironclad 'laurels' such as Portugal laurel (*P. lusitanica*), cherry laurel (*P. laurocerasus*), and its varieties 'Otto Luyken', 'Marbled White', etc (all Z 7–9). All cope with poor, difficult soils and deep shade, but have much more to offer when well grown in sun and decent soil. Abuse them if you must.

RHODODENDRON

The large rhododendron hybrids in a town garden often seem trapped and too vigorous. Better to use species with large foliage, for foliar effect (e.g. *R. rex* and *R. fictolacteum* – both Z 6–11), or to use the small-leaved and small-growing kinds like *R. yakushimanum* and 'Scarlet Wonder' (both Z 5–11). Acid soil is required, and a reasonably moist atmosphere, to keep them happy. Evergreen azaleas can be used to make rolling mounds of low colour.

SKIMMIA

Dense, tough, mounding evergreens, often with scented panicles of flower and, when male and female are present, red berries to follow. Some find skimmias too stolid, but they are invaluable for making low dense mounds in deep shade. Too much sun makes them yellow and chlorotic. Ignore them to your loss. Z 7–9.

VIBURNUM

Too deep a shade stops viburnums flowering as well as they can, though they survive it. Species to look out for are *V. davidii* (ribbed foliage on waist-high domes, male and female needed for the blue berries), *V. tinus* (a medium to large, undistinguished evergreen, but valuable for its toughness and its pink or white flowers which follow on right through the winter and spring) (both Z 7–10), and *V. rhytidophyllum* (a tall species which can be gaunt in heavy shade and has large corrugated foliage) (Z 5–8). Good on alkaline soils.

YUCCA

In full sun there is nothing more dramatic than *Yucca gloriosa* in full flower, that great grey rosette throwing up a candle of creamy bells. Plant it only where the spikes are not too hazardous as you pass (Z 10–11). *Y. filamentosa* is smaller and does not make a trunk (Z 4–10). Both have excellent variegated forms.

Deciduous shrubs

ARALIA ELATA

A tall, suckering shrub with club-like, spiny trunks and long, arching, pinnate foliage topped by white flowers in autumn. It is as dramatic as they come. The variegated form (always grafted) is slower-growing and showier in a more formal situation. Plant it where you can enjoy the winter silhouette. Z 3–10.

CESTRUM PARQUI

A medium-sized, very soft and none too hardy shrub, with willowy leaves and panicles of pale-yellow flowers which are highly perfumed at night. The smell of the bruised foliage is foetid, so plant it where you need not brush against it. A must in the night owl's garden, nevertheless. Sun. Z 8–9.

COTINUS

Smoke bushes do have good autumn colour, but perhaps in a small garden they are more valuable for their "smoke", the candy-floss-like panicles of flower. Be warned: the generosity of their flowering can be very variable. Buy a plant in flower to be sure. Z 5–9.

FICUS CARICA

Figs love city life, and are never happier than when putting roots down into some dry, difficult crack. Give them lots of sun. Train them against a wall, or let them build up into a wide, open shrub. Make the most of that huge, rough foliage. Z 8–11.

HYDRANGEA

If there is enough moisture and food around, the mop-head hydrangeas do well in cities. In city warmth the oak-leaved hydrangea *H. quercifolia* is excellent (Z 5–9), and so is *H. paniculata* (Z 4–9). The taller, hairy-leaved species like *H. aspera* and its subspecies *sargentiana* also prosper and flower well in city warmth, but need cool, shady roots (both Z 5–9). Feed them and mulch them generously to keep them happy.

PAEONIA LUTEA VAR. LUDLOWII

The easiest and most floriferous of the big tree peonies, with large, yellow flowers and bold, pale-green foliage. Plant it with shaded roots and a sunny crown if you can, and keep it well mulched. Be prepared for the stems to arch over as they age, replaced by new stems coming from the base. It needs space, but is worth it. Z 6–9.

PHILADELPHUS 'ERECTUS'

Some consider the mock oranges too crude and vigorous for use in small gardens, despite their perfume. 'Erectus' is worth making the exception. It will produce masses of its small but headily perfumed flowers in a surprising amount of shade, and is totally undemanding as to soil. A necessary filler in any garden. Reaches 1–2m (3–6½ft). Z 5–8.

Cestrum parqui

Climbers

CLEMATIS

Almost every garden will have clematis of some sort. The large-flowered hybrids really are decorative rather than structural, and can be tucked in wherever you wish. But more vigorous species like *C. rehderiana* and *C. montana* (both Z 6–9) can run up into trees, or quickly fill screens to close off a view. The best forms have perfume too. The evergreen but less hardy species *C. armandii* (Z 7–10) comes into its own in the shelter of town gardens.

HEDERA

All gardens need ivy, from the large-leaved variegated *H. colchica* 'Sulphur Heart' (Z 6–9) to black-purple *H. helix* 'Glymii' (Z 5–10). It can be grown on walls or a trellis, or as ground cover under mature trees. *H. canariensis* 'Gloire de Marengo' (Z 8–10) does not self-cling and must have a trellis. Variegated forms are all better in sun.

PARTHENOCISSUS

There are three main species here. *P. quinquefolia*, the Virginia creeper, hauls itself up 15m (50ft) on long tendrils and has great autumn colour (Z 3–10). *P. tricuspidata*, the Boston ivy, clings more tightly to the same height, and colours well (Z 5–10). *P. henryana* has green foliage veined white and is less vigorous and hardy. It hoists itself up on tendrils and colours well in autumn. Good for growing into small trees or deciduous hedges (Z 7–9).

Vitis coignetiae

PILEOSTEGIA VIBURNOIDES

That most sought-after combination – a self-clinging evergreen climber to 6m (20ft) with creamy white flowers in early autumn. Sun or shade. It makes dense cover on the wall, and the flowering growth billows out attractively. It can be kept pruned back to modest proportions, like the climbing hydrangea. Z 7–10.

VITIS

If you like the idea of seeing fruit on a vine, then plant named varieties of the grape vine *Vitis vinifera*, such as 'Brandt' (Z 6–9). If you are more interested in having a bold climber with palmate foliage, then plant *V. coignetiae*, which has huge, corrugated leaves and excellent autumn colour. So long as you prune and pull back every couple of years, you can let it romp into trees and even conifers, without it doing damage (Z 5–9).

WISTERIA

Everyone loves wisteria, but it does need careful control in a small garden, not least to make it flower efficiently. Plant it where you can easily prune it – on a sunny house wall or a pergola. Z 5–9.

Perennials

ACANTHUS

Acanthus is useful for its toughness and ability to grow in difficult soils. Sun makes it flower better, but in hotter climates it performs in shade too. Overfeed it and the stems become too soft and fall over. Once it is established, give it a hard time for best results. Z 6–10.

ANEMONE X HYBRIDA

Japanese anemones are some of the easiest and toughest self-supporting perennials. Heavy soil suits them well, and they cope with drought much better there than on light soils. The white forms will light up a partially shady corner. Z 6–10.

ARUNDO DONAX

For rich, moist soil in sun, there is nothing quite like the great reed to make a 2m (6½ft) pillar of swept-back grey-green foliage. The variegated form is even more striking. It rustles in wind just as well as a bamboo. Z 7–11.

ASPLENIUM SCOLOPENDRIUM

The indispensable hart's tongue fern for cool corners, with strap-like, undivided fronds. The crinkly form 'Crispum' is pure seaweed cast ashore. Plant one in a shady border and wait for others to appear in cracks and crevices nearby. Z 9–11.

BERGENIA

Bergenia will grow almost anywhere, but flowers best in part shade. That simple undivided foliage at ground level is invaluable for foliage contrast. In some forms, such as 'Bressingham Ruby', the winter foliage turns red or purple (Z 3–8). *B. ciliata* is not so hardy, but has larger, hairy leaves (Z 3–10).

BLECHNUM CHILENSE

A wonderful architectural evergreen fern which makes arching billows of hard fronds 60–70cm (24–28in) tall in part shade. In drier soils it will still be happy, but needs to be shadier and cooler. It can look its best in the middle of winter. Z 9–10.

EUPATORIUM PURPUREUM SUBSP. MACULATUM 'ATROPURPUREUM'

A grand performer for a spot which never dries out or gets too hot. Wine-purple stems rise up to 2m (6½ft), topped by flat, purple heads of flower and feathery seedheads to follow. Statuesque to the very end. Butterflies just love it. As good in a cottage garden as in a minimalist garden. Z 4–11.

EUPHORBIA

Euphorbia characias has shrubby stems topped by limy flowers, and makes a striking winter presence. It self-seeds happily into soil or gravels, and can then be moved into suitably sunny positions (Z 7–10). *Euphorbia amygdaloides* var. *robbiae* is a smaller, running species, which flowers in spring above evergreen rosettes. Once it has become established it will colonize dense and even dry shade under trees (Z 8–10).

FUCHSIA

Fuchsias thrive remarkably well in shade, and associate well with ferns to make a good autumn picture. Grow the hardier kinds such as *F. magellanica* and its close hybrids (Z 4–8). In many years the old wood will come through the winter. Some years it will be cut to the ground. In milder climates fuchsias will make arching small trees.

GERANIUM

The hardy geraniums are generally too rampant for a small garden, but there are some which do their spreading from a tight, static crown, and these are most useful. *G. wallichianum* 'Buxton's Variety' makes long arms carrying blue, white-eyed flower in late summer and autumn (Z 4–8). Its hybrid 'Ann Folkard' has even longer arms and its flowers are wine-purple over a much longer season (Z 5–9). *G. renardii* has greeny-grey foliage with chalky flowers in spring, and makes an excellent edging plant (Z 3–10).

GUNNERA MANICATA

Some might think that this "giant rhubarb" is too large for a town garden. But one clump well used can be wonderfully dramatic in the smallest of gardens. It needs cool roots and plenty of moisture, but does not require rich feeding or deep soil. Z 7–11.

HELLEBORUS ORIENTALIS HYBRIDS

These hellebores have such a long season of interest that it is hard to classify them as spring plants. They will live undisturbed for decades in deep shade under trees and shrubs, tight among the roots, and never needing any special attention. The foliage remains good all year. Z 4–10.

HOSTA

Slugs permitting, hostas can make a huge contribution to the lower layers of a garden. There are all colours and habits to choose from, and so long as they are in some shade they will tolerate surprisingly dry conditions. In the warmth of towns,

the white, long-trumpeted, perfumed *H. plantaginea* var. *japonica* is sensational in October. Z 3–9.

OSTEOSPERMUM JUCUNDUM

This soft, aromatic sprawler produces endless white, mauve-backed daisy flowers through the summer, given a reasonably moist soil and sun. In drought it tends to stand still. It is the hardiest of the osteospermums. 'Compactum' is tighter and darker, but not quite so resistant to hard frost. Z 8–11.

PHLOMIS RUSSELIANA

A vigorous spreading plant at ground level with big, heart-shaped leaves. Its yellow flowers rise above, clustered around the stems, which then dry and stand into the winter. Indispensable. Z 4–9.

SEDUM

The large sedums like *S.* 'Autumn Joy', *S.* 'Matrona', and *S. telephium* subsp. *ruprechtii*, are striking throughout the season, from the moment they snout out from the clump to the moment you cut down the dried seedheads in spring. All they ask is sun and reasonably decent soil. All Z 4–10.

VERBENA BONARIENSIS

One of those tall, open-textured, self-supporting flowers of which you can have plenty without them ever seeming heavy. Individual plants do not last long, and it is not very hardy, but they self seed. It can be used as a bedding plant. Butterflies love it. Z 7–10.

Verbena bonariensis *(purple)* and Gaura lindheimeri *(white)*

index

acknowledgments

The artwork on the following pages has been supplied by 52 top Jayne Ford; 67 bottom Julie Toll; 80 left Victor Nelson; 90 left Arabella Lennox-Boyd; 115 right Michèle Osborne; 123 bottom Iris Kaplow; 132 top Jayne Ford.

Photographic acknowledgements in page order
Endpapers Topher Delaney; 1 Jerry Harpur/design: Jeff Mendoza, New York City; 2 Arcaid/Richard Bryant/architect: Peter Aldington; 4–5 Marianne Majerus; 6 Steven Wooster; 7 GettyOne Stone/Stuart Westmorland; 8 Steven Wooster; 9 GettyOne Stone/Michael Busselle; 10 Steven Wooster; 11 Garden Matters; 12 Steven Wooster; 13 Steven Wooster; 14–15 John Glover/design: Tom Cox; 16 Clive Nichols/design: Clare Matthews; 17 John Glover/design: Alan Titchmarsh; 18 Garden Picture Library/Henk Dijkman; 19 top John Glover/design: Chris Jacobsen; 19 bottom Jonathan Buckley/Maurice Green; 20 Mark Schwartz/design: Ron Herman Landscape Architects, www.rherman.com; 21 The Interior Archive/Helen Fickling; 22 Andrew Lawson Photography/design: Christopher Bradley-Hole; 23 The Interior Archive/Helen Fickling/design: Raymond Jungles/Debra Yates; 24 Garden Picture Library/Janet Sorrell; 25 left John Glover/design: Fiona Lawrenson; 25 right Andrew Lawson Photography; 26 Andrew Lawson Photography; 27 John Glover; 28 Garden Picture Library/John Miller; 29 John Glover; 30 Arcaid/Richard Bryant; 31 Jerry Harpur/design: Bradley Dyruff, California; 32 John Glover; 33 John Glover/design: David Andersen; 34 Marianne Majerus/design: Pat Wallace; 35 top Jonathan Buckley; 35 bottom Jerry Harpur/Marcus Harpur; 36 Jerry Harpur/design: Bobbie Hicks, Sydney, Australia; 37 Andrew Lawson Photography; 38 Garden Matters; 39 Jonathan Buckley/design: Paul Kelly; 40 Marianne Majerus/design: Paul Cooper; 41 Marianne Majerus/design: Paul Cooper; 42-43 Jonathan Buckley design: Susan Sharkey; 44 top Will Giles; 44 bottom Topher Delaney; 45 Jerry Harpur/design: Marcia Donohue, Berkeley, California; 46 Marianne Majerus/design: Judy Wiseman; 47 Marianne Majerus/design: Robin Cameron Don; 48 Marianne Majerus/sculpture and design: Camilla Shivarg; 49 John Glover/design: John Simpson; 51 Camera Press/Schöner Wohnen; 52 bottom Jerry Harpur/design: John Wheatman, San Francisco, California; 53 top Jerry Harpur/design: John Wheatman, San Francisco, California; 53 bottom Jerry Harpur/design: John Wheatman, San Francisco, California; 54 Jerry Harpur/photographer: Marcus Harpur; 55 Elizabeth Whiting Associates; 56 Camera Press/Schöner Wohnen; 57 Garden Matters/John Phipps; 58 Jerry Harpur/design: Bob Clark, Oakland, California; 59 Garden Picture Library/Howard Rice; 60 left Will Giles; 60 right Jerry Harpur; 61 Jerry Harpur/design: Dan Pearson/RHS Chelsea Show; 63 Andrea Jones/Andrea Jones Garden Exposures Photo Library; 64 Will Giles; 65 top Marianne Majerus; 65 bottom Will Giles; 66 Andrew Lawson Photography; 67 top Andrew Lawson Photography; 68 top Will Giles; 68 bottom John Glover/design: Geoffrey Whiten; 69 Andrew Lawson Photography; 70 Will Giles; 71 Camera Press/Schöner Wohnen; 72 Marianne Majerus; 73 Jerry Harpur/Cordoba Flower Festival; 74 Will Giles; 75 Jonathan Buckley/design: Declan Buckley; 76 Jerry Harpur/design: Denis Lochen, Jesus Pobre, Spain; 78 Will Giles; 79 Will Giles; 80 right Jerry Harpur/design: Victor Nelson, New York City; 81 top Jerry Harpur/design: Victor Nelson, New York City; 81 bottom Jerry Harpur/design: Victor Nelson, New York City; 82 top John Glover; 82 bottom Elizabeth Whiting Associates; 83 Camera Press/Schöner Wohnen; 84 Camera Press/Schöner Wohnen; 85 Jerry Harpur; 86 top Jerry Harpur/design: Jean Hawkswell, Kent; 86 bottom The Interior Archive /Helen Fickling/ design: Raymond Jungles/Debra Yates; 87 Jerry Harpur/design: Eric Ossart and Arnaud Mauries, Jardin des Paradis, France; 88 Garden Picture Library/design: Hiroshi Nanamori; 89 Jerry Harpur/design Chris Rosmini, Los Angeles, California; 90 right Andrea Jones/Garden Exposures Photo Library/design: Arabella Lennox-Boyd/RHS Chelsea Show; 91 top Andrea Jones /Garden Exposures Photo Library/design: Arabella Lennox-Boyd/RHS Chelsea Show; 91 bottom Jerry Harpur/ design: Arabella Lennox-Boyd/RHS Chelsea Show; 92 Clive Nichols; 93 Arcaid/John Edward Linden/architect: Mark Guard; 94 Jerry Harpur/Ryoan ji Temple, Kyoto, Japan; 95 top Vivian Russell; 95 bottom Andrew Lawson Photography; 96 Andrew Lawson Photography; 97 Marianne Majerus/design: Judy Wiseman; 98 Arcaid/ Richard Bryant/architect: Tadao Ando; 99 The Interior Archive/Helen Fickling/artist: Prinsloo; 100 Clive Nichols/design: Lars Hedstrom, Hedens Lustgard, Sweden; 101 Topher Delaney; 102 John Glover/design: Clarke/Wynniott-Husey; 103 Jerry Harpur/design: Isabelle C Greene, Santa Barbara, California; 104 top Marianne Majerus/design: Christopher Bradley-Hole; 112 Jerry Harpur/design: Luciano Giubbilei, London; 113 Topher Delaney; 114 Marianne Majerus/design: Michèle Osborne; 115 left Marianne Majerus /design: Michèle Osbourne; 116 top Marianne Majerus; 116 bottom Jerry Harpur/design: Stephen Crisp, London; 117 Jerry Harpur/design: Jeff Mendoza, New York City; 118 Andrea Jones/Garden Exposures Photo Library; 119 Jerry Harpur/design: Henrietta Parsons, London; 120 Jerry Harpur /design: Edwina von Gal, New York City; 121 Marianne Majerus; 122 top Jerry Harpur/design: Iris Kaplow, New York City; 122 bottom Jerry Harpur/design: Iris Kaplow, New York City; 123 Jerry Harpur/design: Iris Kaplow, New York City; 124 top John Glover/design: Chris Jacobsen; 124 bottom Elizabeth Whiting Associates; 125 Clive Nichols Garden Pictures/design: Sarah Layton; 127 Garden Picture Library/Ron Sutherland; 128 Elizabeth Whiting Associates; 129 Elizabeth Whiting Associates; 130 John Glover; 131 Jerry Harpur/design: Tim du Val and Dean Payne, New York City; 132 bottom David J Bailey/design: Jayne Ford/ garden construction: Harding Landscapes; 133 top David J Bailey/design: Jayne Ford; Garden construction: Harding Landscapes; 133 bottom David J Bailey/design: Jayne Ford/garden construction: Harding Landscapes; 135 Jerry Harpur/Ron Simple, Pennsylvania; 136 Octopus Publishing Group Ltd./Michael Boys; 139 Andrew Lawson Photography; 140 Andrew Lawson Photography; 141 Beth Chatto, Elmstead Market, Essex/ photographer: Marcus Harpur.